FERRIES
IN SCOTLAND

FERRIES
IN SCOTLAND

MARIE WEIR

JOHN DONALD PUBLISHERS LTD
EDINBURGH

© Marie Weir 1988

ISBN 0 85976 235 1

The publisher acknowledges subsidy from the Scottish Arts Council towards the publication of this volume.

Phototypeset by Pioneer Associates (Graphic) Ltd., Perthshire. Printed in Great Britain by Bell and Bain Ltd., Glasgow.

Acknowledgements

I would like to express my gratitude to the many people who have helped me towards the production of this book. Firstly, I would pay tribute to my mentors Professor Geoffrey Barrow, Department of Scottish History, and Dr. Ian Adam, Department of Geography, both of the University of Edinburgh, for their support and encouragement. I am also greatly indebted to the staffs of the Scottish Record Office, the National Library and the Signet Library, in Edinburgh, together with the many librarians and archivists throughout Scotland for their courteous and knowledgeable service at all times. In addition, I am grateful to those who have kindly permitted me to use their photographs to illustrate the text. Further thanks are due to Mr. John Tuckwell, a most supportive and helpful editor and publisher.

For permission to reproduce illustrations, I should like to thank the following: Aberdeen City Libraries; Aberdeen Journals Ltd; Aberdeen Museum and Art Gallery; the *Illustrated London News*; Inverness Museum and Art Gallery; Mrs MacGregor, 'Wooloomoloo', Garve Road, Ullapool; Captain Murdo Mackenzie, Glenelg; William Mowat, Waulk-mill Cottage, Stormontfield by Perth; Perth Museum and Art Gallery; Pettinain & District SWRI; the *Scotsman*; the Scottish Ethnological Archive, Royal Museum of Scotland; and Mrs C. Turbolt, Petts Wood, Orpington, Kent.

For innumerable discussions, untiring and unstinting support, encouragement and help I am greatly in the debt of Miss J. H. Tiley, MEd.

Finally, for their forbearance, loving understanding and unfailing interest and concern, I thank my mother, my husband and all my family.

Marie Weir
Dunfermline, 1988

Contents

Preface

My interest in Scottish ferries was inspired by watching the Cramond ferry boat plying across the River Almond on the outskirts of Edinburgh. Immediately questions arose probing into the existence of other ferry locations in Scotland, their history, their geographical position, the duration of ferry services, the types of ferry boat, ferry regulations, the life led by ferrymen, the cargoes carried and incidents special to individual ferries. An intensive search revealed a tangled web of information, much of it difficult to trace from a welter of different sources: Acts of Parliament, the Register of the Great Seal, the Statistical Accounts, Agricultural Surveys, Minutes of Commissioners of Supply Committees, Justices of the Peace Committees, Road Trustee Committees, Town Councils, Burgh Councils and related records combined to provide rich primary sources. Furthermore, a wealth of material was to be found in the records of eighteenth- and ninteenth-century travellers including Martin Martin, Richard Franck, Thomas Tucker, Robert Heron, Dr. Johnson, James Boswell, Dorothy Wordsworth, Sarah Murray, James Hogg and Lord Cockburn, the famous circuit judge. Pertinent observations were made by people such as Captain Edward Burt, Sir John Sinclair and John MacCulloch, while views on communication systems were expressed by technical experts including General Wade, General Caulfield, Thomas Telford and Joseph Mitchell.

Ferries, being indispensable to early communications in Scotland, were apt to be taken for granted and attention was paid to them only when problems arose, in which case a mention in the records might be merited. Nevertheless, the development of ferries is so inextricably bound up with national economic and social change that tracing their history

1

inevitably opens up wider perspectives on Scottish life and
culture.

This book explores the story of Scottish ferries over the
last eight hundred years. It does not claim to be comprehensive, particularly as it has not been possible to include ferries
on lochs or canals or those serving Orkney and Shetland.
Conditions encountered on the great variety of waterways
throughout the land, available technological expertise,
sources of funding and the political climate influenced the
design of ferry boats, the management of ferries and the
employment of ferrymen; all these aspects are interwoven.
Ferrymen were a hardy breed and, for many a long year,
took pride in their autonomous position. Their lifestyle over
the centuries is studied in the book together with their
dealings with a wide range of passengers.

In the main, bridges superseded ferries, thus providing an
opportunity for the inclusion of something of the history of
such bridges, culminating in the modern sagas of the great
estuary road bridges. Consideration is also given to the
consolidation in the late twentieth century of the ferry
services to the Western Isles which underpin the economic,
commercial and social life of the islanders.

Ferry steamers to the Western Isles may be the last
survivors of ferry services in Scotland, but nonetheless the
notion of travelling on a ferry has lost none of its appeal.
History and geography, the past and the present, realism
and sentiment all jostle for pride of place in the attentions of
the traveller when journeying on a ferry boat. It is hoped
that readers of this book will, in undertaking their own
search into the history of Scottish ferries and their own
travels on existing ferries, find themselves excited by new
discoveries, fascinated by the impact, the scale and the
methods of ferrying and admiring of the manner in which
ferrymen and travellers alike dealt with almost insurmountable problems.

CHAPTER 1

River Ferries

Throughout Scotland, rivers and burns have always criss-crossed the land-mass, presenting the traveller with the problem of how to proceed from one side to the other. Over the years, different ways have been found to secure crossings. In the seventeenth century, Dollar folk made stilts from tree branches and walked high and dry across the Devon, while Highland women were used as beasts of burden to transport men over slippery, rock-strewn Highland rivers. Ford-women, as they were called, were also in attendance at Border river fords, particularly on fair and market days. More commonly, rivers were forded on horseback, although sudden changes in water levels often made this a hazardous business, with horse and rider not infrequently parting company. Thomas Warden of Dunbar found himself a sorry victim of such an incident in 1517 after a quarrel with David Hume, chief of the Wedderburn clan. Warden escaped on horseback pursued by Hume's page who caught up with him as he crossed the river Whitadder at Broomhouse Ford. Warden's horse stumbled and fell, throwing his unfortunate rider into the water just as two of David Hume's brothers arrived. They slew Warden, cut off his head and carried it to Duns where it was publicly exhibited.

Prior to the seventeenth century, there were at most two hundred bridges in all Scotland. At a time when roads were mainly unmade tracks, bridges were few and far apart and travellers rarely had a convenient or speedy crossing over a river. Public clamour did sometimes result in the erection of a new bridge, although general investment in bridge building did not begin in earnest until the beginning of the nineteenth century. Consequently, until the proliferation of bridge building in the eighteenth century, fording and ferry boats offered the only alternative means of crossing rivers.

The image surrounding river ferries, especially in the eighteenth and nineteenth centuries, is frequently enhanced by fantasies of life styles, long lost, and to be envied in contrast to the hustle of twentieth century living. In reality, life for ferrymen was hard. It was different for the ferry proprietors, usually influential, wealthy landowners, who rented out the right of ferry to whichever cottar offered the highest bid. In the 1770s, the Duke of Gordon demonstrated this kind of financial acumen in relation to the let of the ferry at Fochabers. On 3rd February, Alex Brogue offered £39 Stg for the let; on 24th February, John Robertson submitted a bid of £43 Stg; on 3rd March, William Bell bid £45 Stg. The Duke leaked the information regarding the amounts contained in these offers, so, on 7th May, John Robertson increased his first bid to £52 Stg but the Duke finally made the best deal on 26th May when he accepted an offer of £53 Stg from John Gordon who was duly awarded the ferry tack. A ferry proprietor expected payment in kind as well as in cash. Therefore, John Gordon's contract stated that the ferryman would, in addition to the cash paid, supply '4 bolls and i firlot of clean oatmeal and bere'. He also promised to 'serve the passage readily and pleasantly at all times and never to exact above the fares that have been established at the ferry by his Grace'. Furthermore, a ferry proprietor benefited by free passage being given at all times to himself, his family, servants and friends. However, there were compensations for the ferryman. A rent-free cottage and surrounding ground were included in the ferry tack or let. This cottage could serve a dual purpose, both as a dwelling house and as an inn. Thus, a crude form of hospitality was provided for travellers while the ferryman was able to increase his income. The most expensive outlay for the ferryman was the necessity of keeping 'a good and sufficient' boat especially as more than one boat could be involved. Boats were often damaged by spates, rocks or

In the mid-eighteenth century, women, known as 'ford women', transported passengers and goods from ferry boats to the land. Captain Burt described how 'At low ebb, when their Boats lie off at a considerable Distance from the Shore, for Want of Depth of Water, the Women tuck up their Garments to an indecent Height and wade to the Vessels . . . .'

simply wear and tear. Occasionally, at the most frequented ferries, financial help was given to the ferrymen. In 1662, for example, the 'baillies and counsell' of Lanark were 'content to give to the botteris at Thankerton, to help build the boatt, ten merks Scots'.

Military strategy sometimes involved the destruction of ferry boats as ferry crossings could be of strategic importance.

This was true during the 1715 and 1745 Jacobite uprisings. In August 1745, General Sir John Cope (Johnnie Cope of the famous ballad), was marching upon the barracks at Ruthven, near Kingussie. He came upon the ferry boat on the river Spey near Ruthven which served the garrison there. The General ordered his artillery to destroy the ferry boat. Consequently, the ferry service could not function again for the next two years. Such military intervention was infrequent and ferrymen with licence to ferry on a river were virtually autonomous, in spite of the fact that legislation regulated ferry services. Implementation of acts or decrees was difficult although Justices of the Peace and Commissioners of Supply had been amalgamated as early as 1686 for the very purpose of strengthening control over ferry and other services. The ferryman was the man on the spot and passengers were at his mercy as in the case of the ferryman at Balmackneill on the Tay near Dunkeld in 1731. The farmer, James Robertson, wished to catch the weekly post to Edinburgh with a letter of great importance. On arrival at Balmackneill, on the opposite side to the ferryman's cottage, he hallooed for a long time but neither the ferryman nor his wife chose to pay any attention. Angry and frustrated, Robertson then hurried to Logierait, the next ferry crossing on the Tay, by which time the post had departed, leaving him to wait for another week before his letter could be sent.

The right of ferry on rivers was mainly held by individual landowners although at a few locations this right was held by the local town council, as was the case at Perth. Of course, the demand for a ferry service there was relatively sudden. It occurred when the bridge across the Tay finally collapsed in 1621 and the Town Council had to respond to the public need for immediate transportation across the river. At the same period, the magistrates of Annan held the right to ferry across the Water of Annan. They were forced to take action against eight burgesses who tried to obstruct the ferry boat. This produced an outcry over the loss of traffic travelling northwards into Scotland and westwards to Ireland. The

The ferry boat on the passage over the Tweed at Kelso in the eighteenth century. The cargo of two horses appear to be free standing in the stern of the boat, thus illustrating the hazardous nature of ferrying at that time.

public were only appeased when the eight men were imprisoned. At Irvine, too, the Town Council, proprietors of the ferry across the River Irvine, contributed towards the upkeep of the ferry boat. This may have shown a concern for the safety of the public but it also demonstrated an awareness of the need to keep the passage open in order to collect the dues from a steady flow of travellers moving to and from the west-coast ports. This consistent source of revenue was not to be abandoned lightly.

Since the majority of travellers approach Scotland from the south, it seems logical to pursue a south to north route in order to convey a picture of ferry life in Scotland over the years. The traveller into southern Scotland has always been faced by a matrix of natural barriers. A series of formidable rivers bar the way from south to north and from east to west. It is no wonder that marauding invaders from the Romans to the Roundheads expended as much energy in attempting to establish routes of communication as they did in striving to overcome the doughty defence of the Scottish forces. Before the Union of the Crowns in 1603, and for some time afterwards, it was a daunting prospect for any traveller to make his way even from the Border area to Edinburgh. The most frequented route, avoiding the main hazards of bog, river and hill, hugged the east coast from Berwick. Although parish roads did exist, they were commonly formed by usage rather than by any attempt at formal construction. In the seventeenth century coaches and carriages were virtually unknown and only the well-to-do rode; the rest walked. Carts were a rare sight and goods were transported on horseback in sacks or creels. Under such conditions the time taken to complete journeys was measured in weeks rather than in days and certainly not in hours. It took two weeks for a common carrier, using a single horse to pull a crude cart, to complete the journey between Selkirk and Edinburgh, a distance of thirty-eight miles. On the roads of today, the same carrier, using motor transport, might expect to arrive in Edinburgh in under two hours.

Prior to the seventeenth century, lack of bridges increased the length of the journey. Even at Berwick, those crossing the Tweed, between 1294 and 1376, were dependent on a ferry service where the rights of ferry were divided between the king and the Pope. The only bridge over the Tweed then was a poor timber construction at Peebles, a popular summer holiday residence for early kings of Scotland where they pursued rural diversions. No doubt the constant presence of royalty, their courts and fringe attendants, greatly increased the volume of traffic over the fragile bridge and hastened the erection of a second, more substantial, stone-built bridge. This was completed in the fifteenth century and was known as the Bridge of Tweed. The people of Peebles were expected

In the 1890s, the Lampits chain ferry boat on the Clyde near Carnwath was easily operated by the ferryman and sometimes by his wife or daughter. The nearby Ferry Cottage was conveniently situated for waiting passengers.

to provide labour to erect the bridge but incentives were offered to make the job more attractive. Workers, such as Wat Fylder and Kate Walwood, were made burgesses of the town for carrying 'loads of stones for the bridge'.

By the mid-eighteenth century, town councils had become less philanthropic and Kelso Town Council, far from rewarding the efforts of the citizens when they contributed towards the building of a bridge, imposed an additional tax. A duty extracted 'two Pennies Scots or one-sixth part of every Penny Sterling upon every Scots pint of Ale, Porter or Bear which shall be brewed for Sale, brought into, tapped or sold with the town of Kelso'. Unfortunately, in 1793, a flood destroyed the Kelso bridge and travellers and citizens once again had to cross the Tweed by ferry. In 1803, John Rennie gave priority to rebuilding the bridge and was so pleased with the result that he later used the design as a prototype for the old Waterloo Bridge in London. When Waterloo Bridge was dismantled in 1934 two lamps were taken to Kelso and they were erected on the bridge where they can be seen today.

The River Tweed, the longest and most important river in the Borders, is famous for the Abbeys of Kelso, Dryburgh and Melrose sited on or near its banks. Although the Abbey communities were self-contained, travellers were constantly coming and going. Royalty, churchmen, academics, merchants, local dignitaries and others had all to be transported over the Tweed by ferry. Castles are scattered throughout the Borders and access to them was often made by ferry. For example, many important personages used the ferry to reach the castle of Wark on the River Tweed, near Coldstream. In 1296, Edward I visited the castle. He was captivated by a fellow guest, the beautiful Countess of Sutherland. When they were alighting from the ferry boat which had carried them across the Tweed on an excursion, the Countess dropped her garter before the King. He picked it up and gallantly returned it to her saying, 'Honi soit qui mal y pense', thus, it is said, instituting the Order of the Garter.

In the fifteenth century, Pope Pius II, while visiting northern Britain, disguised himself as a merchant and arrived at Wark. The Pope used the ferry in order to visit a peasant farmer's cottage to find out how the poor of the country lived. According to custom, the farmer gave this stranger hospitality and was astonished when the man brought out wines and relishes from his bag, luxuries unknown to a poverty-stricken peasant. Norham, another castle not far from Wark, could be approached by fords but at the nearby village of Ladykirk a ferry plied the river. It was here, in 1505, that James IV found himself in grave danger of his life as he crossed the water in the midst of a tumultuous spate. So grateful was he to survive that he built a church at Ladykirk and had an inscription inserted above the church door. Later, a bridge was built at Norham and in 1884, a Tweed Bridges Trust was formed to oversee the

Slezer's print, 1678, showed a ferry boat on the passage over the Tay at Perth. Perth was without a bridge across the river for a period of 150 years.

administration of the bridges at Norham, Coldstream and the Union Chain bridge near Berwick. The Trust, composed of representatives from both sides of the border, carried out these duties successfully and without comment until 1987 when an impasse was reached. The three Scottish represent-atives considered that the Trust had outlived its usefulness but the three English trustees opposed this view. As a result, Northumberland County Council Highways and Transport Committee intervened and commented that they saw no reason at this point why the Trust should be wound up.

There was an ancient ferry on the Tweed at Boleside or Boldside situated about a quarter of a mile west of Abbotsford, the residence of Sir Walter Scott. Boldside had gained some importance in connection with the adoption of a plum tree on the armorial bearings of Galashiels. In 1337, during the invasion of Scotland by Edward III, an event occurred which gave rise to the use of this symbol. A party of English soldiers, encamped near Galashiels, wandered through the surrounding woods in search of wild plums. Citizens of the town ambushed the invaders at Boldside and

cut them down to a man. The victorious Scots, jubilant that
the fruit resulting from the Englishmen's search had proved
to be a great deal more sour than they had anticipated,
dubbed themselves 'The soor plooms of Galashiels', and
from that time a plum tree was incorporated into the
Galashiels crest.

From time to time, especially in early winter, the Tweed
floods. These spates made navigation difficult for ferrymen
and occasionally accidents happened. In 1723, at Boleside,
on the third Wednesday of November, Martinmas Fair day,
a tragedy occurred. Roads leading to and from the town
were crowded with people and beasts. Money changed hands,
as servants were bent on 'laying out their wages before they
entered service again'. Ale was in great demand as the
holiday spirit was kindled. It was a day to be enjoyed. That
Wednesday was chosen as the wedding day for a young
farmer and his bride. They travelled to Galashiels for the
marriage ceremony together with their family and friends.
All day they celebrated and in the evening they were
returning home via the Boleside ferry. The boat, large,
broad-beamed, unwieldy and open, was propelled by the
ferryman who sat near the prow and manipulated two long
pole-like oars. The level of the river was high and a strong
current tugged fiercely at the boat as it set out for the
opposite side. The normal width of the passage, about two
hundred and fifty yards, was greatly increased by the
flooding which also made embarking and disembarking
difficult and dangerous. When all the passengers, together
with one horse, were safely aboard the ferryman pushed the
boat into the river. The over-loaded vessel made its way
slowly across the passage with the ferryman struggling to
control it. As it approached the south bank the ferryman
threw a rope to waiting by-standers and managed to scramble
ashore. The rope was twisted around a tree stump but it
became so taut that when the boat jerked it snapped. The boat
was swept away and drifted helplessly, with the passengers
panicking. Suddenly, the boat capsized with men, women

This tombstone in memory of John Duff whose family had been ferrymen at Perth for generations, depicts the small type of boat he used. He was ninety-eight years old when he died in 1772 only one year after the opening of the new bridge at Perth.

and children struggling and screaming in the cold water. The horse proved to be a life-saver as some people were saved by holding on to its tail and mane. Others, less lucky, were drowned, including the newly-wed couple and their attendants. Out of the thirty-three people on board, only fifteen were saved.

One young man, named Williamson, had a miraculous escape. In the first instance, when he was thrown into the water, he was able to cling to a sack filled with 'Galashiels Gray' cloth and thus managed to keep himself afloat. However, this buoy became saturated with water but at this point a wooden spar, part of the broken boat, came within his reach. He grasped the wood to his chest and in this manner he was carried downstream. He managed to survive the current as it swirled him between the pillars of an ancient, ruined bridge. He was carried along the course of the river for about three miles before being rescued by the quick-thinking action of a young ploughman who had been a horrified witness of the accident. Standing on the south bank at Boldside, this young man had the presence of mind to catch the horse that had been on the ferry boat as the animal reached the bank. He mounted the horse and galloped along the south bank of the River Tweed to try to reach the next ferry location as quickly as possible. Arriving at Westhouses ferry, where a ferry boat was tied, he dismounted and, together with the ferryman, launched the boat. They were just in time to rescue Williamson who was still clutching the piece of wood. Williamson venerated that wooden spar to such an extent that when he died in 1763 it was buried with him. He had left instructions that the wood was to form part of his coffin. It was commonly thought that the cause of the disaster was bound up with witchcraft. Soon afterwards an old woman confessed to being with the 'Evil One' at the time of the accident. She said that together, in the guise of 'twa corbies', they had sat on the bow of the doomed boat and cast spells. Later the 'Evil One' had treated the old woman to 'the fattest haggis' she had ever seen. Unfortunately, records do not relate her fate.

Today, visitors to Abbotsford can wander down to the edge of the Tweed and look upstream to where the Boldside ferry was once located. On a tranquil summer day, with the smooth waters of the river gently lapping the grass edges, it is difficult to imagine the noise and the horror of that gloomy November evening in 1723. Yet it is not surprising that the Boldside ferry passage has been labelled 'The Dead Water' since that fateful night.

In days when superstition prevailed, drowning was often regarded as retribution. In 1707, a curious view was taken regarding the drowning of the eldest son of Sir William Maxwell of Monrieth, Wigtownshire at the ferry crossing the river Nith near Dumfries. Father and son had quarrelled and the son was on his way to Edinburgh to petition against

The Waulkmill ferry passage over the Tay was served by two boats. The twin-hulled, pontoon-type ferry boat, propelled by the use of a chain and cogwheel, operated from the mid-nineteenth century. These can be seen on the left of the boat. In the foreground the small ferry boat is about to depart with three passengers.

the father. The report on the accident comments,' . . . people generally say the father was in the wrong . . . so they look upon the drowning as no particular judgement on the son'. However, in 1730, one enterprising burgess in Kirkcud-brightshire took an initiative to protect his own safety and the wellbeing of others. Quintin Maclung, a tailor, lived beside the influx of a 'large burn, the Paharoow', into the River Dee. Daily he had to ferry across this water as he carried out his business, and in so doing he often feared for his life. He resolved to protect others from similar risks. Maclung's earnings were never more than 4d a day but somehow he managed to save enough to pay to have a bridge erected. A large stone remains from that bridge and on it Quintin Maclung's name is inscribed as a testimony to his

public spirit. Almost two hundred years later, bridge-
building expanded in the Borders to meet the needs of
wheeled vehicles and changing expectations regarding speed
and ease of travel. The advent of steam, the development of
the railways and the innovation of the motor car combined
to make the ferries redundant in this area. Nevertheless,
ancient ferry sites can be located without too much difficulty
and it is possible to envisage crossings in days when pressure
of time was an inconvenience rather than a catastrophe.

Moving northwards towards the central area of Scotland,
the Clyde is the next river encountered by the traveller. At
first, the Clyde follows a northerly course, thus presenting a
barrier to those travelling east and west. There is little
agreement regarding the precise spot where the river ends
and the estuary begins but for the purpose of this book that
point is taken to be at Glasgow. The Clyde, rising from the
water of Daer in the Lowther hills, winds its way towards
Glasgow. This is a commercial river set in a fertile, verdant
valley where agriculture was always a major influence. In
addition, the excavation of lead in the sixteenth and
seventeenth centuries at Leadhills provided an alternative
source of income and occupation which was reinforced by
the opening up of the Lanarkshire coalfields in the
eighteenth and nineteenth centuries. Furthermore, the Clyde
intersected the great east-west routes of the country. Roads
between Edinburgh and Glasgow, Edinburgh and Ayr and
long-established ways from the south including those from
Carlisle and Dumfries to Glasgow all passed over the Clyde
at some point. The prosperous nature of Strathclyde dictated
considerable local movement between Biggar, Lanark,
Peebles, Kilmarnock and Hamilton. In view of all this
activity, crossings over the Clyde were crucial. A combination
of fords, ferries and bridges proved to be reasonably effective
but industrial and social change in the late eighteenth and
nineteenth centuries provided strong enough incentives for
money to be invested in the building of bridges, and

On a warm day in the summer of 1912 Davie Rutherford, the ferryman, can be seen rowing a young lady over the Tay at Waulkmill. In the background lies the larger, twin-hulled ferryboat overlooked by the ferryman's cottage.

although ferries were eventually superseded, their importance cannot be overestimated.

The Clydesholm ford and ferry was one of the major ferry locations on the Clyde. It was situated on a bend of the river near to the village of Kirkfield and only half a mile from the town of Lanark. It lay on the route taken by travellers going to and from Lothian, Ayrshire and Galloway, in addition to local people passing and re-passing to Lanark. The first mention of a ferry boat at Clydeholm is a reference dated 7th March 1491 on a charter of James IV granting a right to ferry. The right to ferry was being acknowledged because one of the king's 'familiar knights', Sir Stephen Lockhart of

Cleghorn, patron of the altar of St. Katherine's in the chapel
of St. Nicholas in Lanark, told the king that a ferry at
Clydeholm was essential to convey the 'lieges of the king'
who daily assembled there in great numbers and were often
'imperilled and perished'. The King agreed to the establishment of a ferry but four years later, in 1495, the ferryman,
John Ramage, was accused of 'wrangis uptaking and
withholding of v merkis' on the ferry. He was found guilty
and duly dismissed, although this incident did not affect the
continuation of the ferry. In 1553, the remuneration to John
Hastie, the ferryman at Clydeholm, consisted of 'hous, yardis,
four soumis of gers [a soum equals pasture for one cow or
five sheep] with half the profit of the bait' under payment to
the chaplain of the altar of St. Katherine 'yearly of fyf markis
and four pennis gud and usual mony of the realm'. Each
ferryman also contracted to 'byg, bait and uphold the half of
the said bait with the hous that he duellis in, laying down
penne for penne in all necessar thynges perteyning to the
said bait'.

Two families, the Hasties and the Pomphreys, father
succeeded by son, remained the ferrymen at Clydesholm
until a bridge was built in 1699. At that time, the ferrymen
received compensation of 100 merks for the loss of earnings.
James Pomphrey, the last ferryman, was a dour character
who stood against the authority of Lanark Town Council in
1716 after he had been made redundant. He decided to build
a house and produced a charter proving he owned land
giving access to the horse market, an important mart in
Lanark attended by traders from all over Scotland.
Pomphrey was oblivious to pleas to reconsider his plans
until the Town Council paid him the compensation he was
seeking. Then he built a house elsewhere.

Another ancient ferry over the Clyde was the passage
called Crookboat. This was well-named as it was located on a
sharp loop of the river directly above the confluence of the
Clyde and the Douglas water south of Lanark. In 1671, it is
recorded that 'the Baillies and Counsell is content to give to

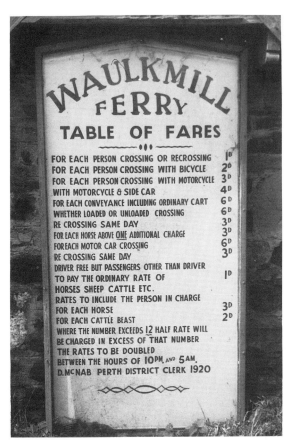

This board incorporates the 1920 table of ferry fares at the Waulkmill crossing for both the large and the small boats and can be seen below the ferryman's cottage on the north bank of the Tay.

the botteris of Cruik-Boatt ten punds Scots to make up ane neu bait . . .'. The burgh of Lanark had a particular interest in preserving this ferry as it was by this route that loads of peat and coal were transported to the town from the Douglas pits and moors. In 1717, Sir James Carmichael, laird of Bonnington, the estate on which the Crookboat ferry was situated, decided to close the access road to the ferry. This road was part of an avenue leading to his mansion house of Bonnington and he resented the invasion of his privacy by the ferry-going public. The decision caused great consternation and Lanark Town Council appealed to the laird to reconsider in the light of the public good and of the loss of revenue to the town from the lack of ferry fares. Eventually, Sir James acquiesced and the Crookboat ferry remained open until the demand for it died naturally in the eighteenth century.

About three miles north of Lanark, the river could be crossed at the Crossford ferry, which operated well into the nineteenth century. In common with other ferries in Scotland, the ferrymen came from generations of the same family. In the 1720s and 1730s, the Jacks were the ferrymen. They were succeeded, in the 1740s, by the Clellands and the Martins, with the ferry licence being taken by the Lockhart family in the 1750s and 1760s. In 1817, a descendant of the Martin family, Archibald Martin, resurrected the right to ferry at Crossford as this had fallen into disuse for the previous thirty or so years. At the same time, a neighbour, John Thomson, set up a rival ferry boat downriver from Crossford. It appeared that Thomson held fishing rights for that stretch of water but not ferry rights. However, this did not deter him from carrying out a ferry service and receiving payment. Martin objected as the ferry rights had been included in his purchase of land in 1809, so he petitioned the Court of Session. The verdict in favour of Martin was based on the precedent established in the Tarbet v Bogle case whereby in law fishing right had no equivalent right of ferry. Consequently, Martin was left unmolested to provide a ferry service for the public at Crossford.

The last river ferry to operate on the Clyde was the Lampits ferry at Pettinain at a point on the river that was subjected to frequent intensive flooding. Pettinain was central to routes from the south leading to Carnwath, Carstairs and Lanark. In the first decades of the nineteenth century, improved methods of agriculture resulted in more

The ferry boat at Burnbank, near Stanley, on the Tay in the 1890s, is an example of the relatively simple modifications carried out on existing boats to enable them to meet the increasing demands for transporting bulky agricultural goods and vehicles. The broad-beamed base of the boat, supporting a spacious platform, was propelled by a chain and fly-wheels and easily manned.

local products being transported to nearby markets. Therefore the number of carts greatly increased while, at the same time, there were more coaches and carriages. The transport of these vehicles across the Clyde began to create difficulties, so in 1840 a number of wealthy, public-spirited landowners subscribed £500 towards a new design of ferry boat to be put on the river at Pettinain. This boat took the form of a float attached to a chain cable stretched across the water passage and was said to be 'so easily worked that a boy can manage it'. It was capable of transporting cattle and all kinds of carriages, and 'holds four carts at one time', which proved to be a great asset until 1905. The replacement, costing £400, was an even better boat which supplied the passage until the 1920s.

Ferries no longer ply the River Clyde but the many bridges built to replace them still stand, albeit reinforced to carry modern traffic. Although, nowadays, passage over these bridges is free, in 1663, tolls were extracted. Tolls at the Clyde and Duneaton bridges included 'For every horse and load, 12 pennies Scots; for every horse and cow, 8 pennies; for every sheep 2 pennies; for every single horseman, 6 pennies and for each footman, 2 pennies'.

In comparison with the Clyde, the River Forth had little in its favour in commercial, social or even aesthetic terms. From its source, west of Aberfoyle, to Stirling when it becomes tidal, the Forth winds in and out of bogs and mosses. Few villages were sustained by it. Crossing this river, as it flows from west to east, was hazardous enough but the demand was too small to make the provision of ferries a viable proposition. Boats may have been used but only ferries at Drip, Badd, Killbeg, Frew and Gartarten are mentioned in the records. The ferry at Drip, half-a-mile west of Stirling, was perceived to be of some strategic value. In 1715, the ferryman, John McFeat, was paid £2/2/— Scots weekly to guard the ferry boat and to report any suspicious characters loitering nearby. McFeat also had the occupation of 'chopman', so he evidently possessed the appropriate credentials as a spy. Later, in more peaceful times, this ferry was used to transport lime when Lord Kaimes of Blairdrummond attempted to improve the land. Finally, a bridge was erected in 1782.

From earliest times, the most important crossing over the Forth was at Stirling. The Romans erected a wooden bridge adjacent to a ford which, in 1297, was used to advantage by William Wallace who won a famous victory over the English there. English soldiers were ambushed as they filed across the narrow bridge which allowed only a few to pass at a time. The bridge, of course, was destroyed and this proved to be of great inconvenience to the local population. Ferry boats had to be used for the next hundred years until a stone bridge

Special landing platforms were designed to operate in conjunction with chain-driven ferry boats. At Caputh on the Tay in the 1890s a pony and trap is about to drive off the ferryboat with the driver remaining in his seat for the whole journey, thus saving time and effort.

was built in the fifteenth century, and this remained intact until after the battle of Sheriffmuir in 1715, when retreating government troops destroyed one of the arches which was not repaired for some years. By 1736, the narrowness of the structure was causing considerable problems as carts with 'heavy carriadges' found difficulties in passing over it, thus causing great delays. In 1745, during the second Jacobite uprising, another arch was destroyed on the orders of Major-General Blackney, commander of Stirling castle. Again, ferry boats were employed until the bridge was repaired. In 1826, a new bridge was completed although the ford was still occasionally used prior to the completion of a second modern bridge.

For the bygone traveller journeying northwards after

crossing the Forth, the Rivers Earn and Tay beckoned, promising little more in ease of passage but guaranteeing beautiful scenery. Like the Clyde and the Forth, the first bridges were built at vital points, at Bridge of Earn and at Perth. In 1326, Robert the Bruce foresaw the need for two stone bridges over the Earn and the Tay respectively; the stone came from local quarries belonging to Scone Abbey. However, the tale of the two bridges over the Earn and the Tay was one of the 'pends and bows falling down, being evil bigged from the beginning, filled only with clay and earth and without any blind pends . . .'. The need for a bridge at Perth in particular was recognised by James VI as '. . . a most precious jewil in our kingdom and a work profitable and primely necessary to our whole kingdom and dominion . . . for the suppression of rebels . . . and also keeping the one-half of the kingdom with the other half in faith, obedience, duty and office towards us, their king . . .'. Payments were constantly being made, according to the Exchequer Rolls, towards the repair and renewal of the fabric of both bridges but boats were kept in readiness for the times when the bridges were under repair.

At Perth, the bridge over the Tay was finally demolished in 1621. For the next 150 years the passage was served by thirty boats and almost as many ferrymen. The ferrymen, in common with most of their kind in Scotland at that time, lived on the farther shore of the passage, at Bridge-end. At first, many boatmen capitalised on the public need for transportation across the river and boats sailed without licence or authority. Perth Town Council, aware of the loss of revenue and the lack of regulations, issued a series of local acts aimed at making the ferrymen more accountable. As there was no tacksman to employ a supervisor, these acts were not enforced and the ferrymen continued to please themselves. By the 1730s, some regulations were establishd, mainly by custom and wont. It became accepted, for example that the ferrymen would provide a service from 5am to 10pm between April and September and from 7am to 8pm during

In 1903, the Caputh crossing over the Tay was sufficiently busy to justify a passenger rowing boat and a twin-hulled, chain-driven boat for horse-drawn vehicles. The ferryman lived in the white house on the north bank. In earlier days, this had also served as an inn providing hospitality for waiting passengers.

the rest of the year. A ferryman's work was arduous and best suited to young men. In 1770, the average age of ferrymen at Perth was nineteen years. However, as these men enjoyed continuous lifelong employment, the average age rose to sixty-four years by 1765, with an equivalent fall in the standard for the ferry service. By that time, pressure to build a bridge had greatly increased. The influential Earl of Kinnoull added his weight to the arguments and proved to be particularly persuasive as he promised to provide considerable financial backing for the project. As a result, a new bridge, designed by John Smeaton, was opened in 1771. To commemorate the occasion, a half-penny coin was struck depicting a ferryman standing beside his coble.

Thirteen ferry locations have been identified on the River

Tay between Perth and Kenmore and that number is probably not comprehensive. Inevitably, legal wranglings arose from time to time regarding the interpretation of ferry rights. The ferry at Kincarrathie was not infrequently the subject of petitions and counter petitions. The Kincarrathie ferry, on the west bank of the river below Stormontfield, operated to the head of the North Inch on the west bank. This was a favourite ferry with cattle drovers as it was easy for the cattle to swim across while the drovers used the boat. Problems arose when large numbers of cattle, after landing, roamed freely over the Inch. The citizens of Perth objected to the desecration of the land they kept for pleasure and leisure. In 1735, the Town Council acted forcibly to improve matters and authorised that the ferry boats be destroyed, oars smashed and the ferrymen imprisoned. However, reference to the charter of 1536, which granted the right of ferry 'without obstruction or molestation', resulted in the Town Council having to retract. Ferry boats were reinstated although limitations were put on the transportation of cattle. In 1771, the opening of Perth bridge attracted traffic previously accommodated by Kincarrathie ferry, so it fell into disuse.

In 1877, the Waulkmill ferry rights were likewise in dispute. Waulkmill ferry passengers had, from time immemorial, landed at the 'waulk-mill of Innerbuist' on the east bank and on the 'lands of Hatton' on the west bank. Until 1877, the two landowners, the Earl of Mansfield and Mr. Maxtone Graham respectively, seemed to have co-operated satisfactorily but when the Earl introduced a twin-hulled, chain-propelled boat, difficulties arose. The chain had to be attached to a post 'to be fixed in the soil of the land of Hatton'. Mr. Maxtone Graham questioned the Earl's right to do this. After a legal wrangle, a previous act of 1811 established sufficient precedent to enable the Earl to carry out his improvements without fear of harassment. In 1891, this new boat was again the centre of contention. During a spate, the cargo of two horses and carts was swept away.

John Slezer drew this print of 'The Prospect of the Town of Dunkeld' in 1678. It shows ferryboats on the East passing over the Tay at Dunkeld. The ferrymen stood upright in their boats and wielded a long, simple oar in such a manner as to harness the strong currents and facilitate as easy a crossing as possible.

Compensation was claimed by the owners. The value of the horses was £120, the cart wheels £3/15/— and the salvaging of a cart and harness £1/5/—. The total bill, including other items, amounted to £136-17-2d. The ferry continued until 1964 when the ferryman, being seventy-four years old, wished to retire, so it was replaced by a cheaper, more convenient bus service. The ferryman's attractive cottage on the east bank is still occupied. A 1929 tarriff of ferry fares is displayed and the access roads to the ferry landing places can be clearly seen.

Nearly five miles upstream, Burnbank ferry was much in demand in the 1890s when the cotton-spinning mills of Stanley were flourishing. Further north on the Tay the ferry locations of Kinclaven, Caputh and Dunkeld all had strong links with the church. The bishops of Dunkeld, from the thirteenth century, were a power in the land and most of them were committed to building a bridge at Dunkeld. For over a hundred years there was a great struggle to achieve this. Money, time and labour were liberally spent but the technology for successful bridge-building was insufficient. At that period, bridges were constructed with huge, broad-based piers which, by their very bulk, built up an enormous pressure of water. This, in turn, resulted in the destruction of the piers as they could not withstand the pressure, so the bridge collapsed. However, the bishops of Dunkeld persevered, using at one time, 947 horses, some carrying lime from Perth, at a cost of £27-7-5d Scots, others carting 932 loads of clay and 2,500 loads of wall stones. Boys were employed to 'watch the ford for a flood' and to 'gather withies to make baskets and barrows'. In 1512, new stables were built at Dunkeld and Caputh to house additional horses. The bill was met by the bishops who also paid the wages of the ferrymen. Eventually, defeat had to be admitted and bridge-building abandoned, so ferries were used to cross the Tay at Dunkeld until early in the nineteenth century.

The churches at Caputh and Kinclaven came within the diocese of Dunkeld, so those attending services on a Sunday had to be transported across the river. In medieval times, a castle stood at Kinclaven and the comings and goings in connection with it required the services of a ferry. An 'excellent inn', doubling as the ferryman's house, stood adjacent to the ferry but hospitality was less necessary in the late nineteenth century when the ferry boat was twin-hulled and chain-propelled, permitting carriages and carts to drive on and off without unhitching the horses, thus minimising delays. A famous passenger used this ferry in 1905 when Elizabeth, the Queen Mother, was taken across as a child to attend a service at Kinclaven church. Later that year, a stone bridge superseded the ferry. Even at the present time, the ferry is missed by worshippers as the division of the land by the river obliges villagers to travel at least two miles by road to reach the church, instead of a five-minute ferry journey. It costs approximately £150 per annum to bus children to the church each Sunday.

J.C. Nattes print of Dunkeld, 1747, depicts the ferryboat on the East passage over the Tay at Dunkeld. Although no quays were provided for the convenience of ferry passengers at this time, a slipway on the north bank is evident, thus providing easy access from the road leading into Dunkeld.

Caputh ferry, similar to the crossing at Kinclaven, served a principally agricultural community. When improvements in agriculture resulted in increased produce, more and bigger carts were required, so the volume of traffic at Caputh increased. As the eighteenth century progressed, the ferrymen devised a procedure for the loading of carts. Four men were required. One held the empty shafts; two were stood by the wheels; and the fourth man supervised. The boatman, standing between the shafts, perched on the furthest lip of the boat to balance the cart on two narrow planks of wood resting on the bulwarks. If the two men at the wheels allowed the cart to dip suddenly into the bottom of the boat, the man holding the shafts was likely to be catapulted into the water. Carters often indulged in racing each other to see who would reach the ferry first. It was commonplace for as many as fourteen carts to queue up to await the ferry, which illustrates what a busy place it must have been. Caputh, too, benefited from the new type of boat being used for river ferry passages in the nineteenth century. In the 1830s, James Fraser, a blacksmith from Dowally, on the north side of Dunkeld, designed a pontoon-type boat for the ferry passage at Caputh. The ferryman, John Ferguson, boasted that 'I have, in my time, sailed mair than mony times the distance round the world, an' that is mair ower fresh water than some, wha caas themselves sailors hae douone ower saut'. An iron bridge, built in 1897, stands over the ferry passage at Caputh and the ferryman's house still overlooks the water. The chain which used to drive the boat now decorates the walls surrounding a house in Caputh village. The old slipway stones, too, can easily be distinguished on each side of the ferry passage.

Dunkeld dominated the strath of Tay. The early establishment of the church, the garrisoning of troops, the great fairs and markets and, in the eighteenth century, the building of Wade's roads combined to give the town status and importance. Routes from Perth and the south, from Blairgowrie and the east, from Pitlochry and the north and from Crieff and the west centred on Dunkeld. Yet, in spite of its being the focus of communication no bridge was built until 1809 when Thomas Telford was employed to erect the bridge that still stands over the Tay to this day. Crossings were made only by ferry boat until then. Three ferries, all ancient locations, were situated near the town, the east and west ferries over the Tay and the ferry at Inver over the River Bran. The Inver ferry was a less busy crossing than those at Dunkeld but it was popular with travellers who wished to visit the inn there. The famous Neil Gow, a celebrated self-taught fiddler and native of Inver, was patronised by the Duke of Atholl. People flocked to hear

Telford's toll bridge over the Tay at Dunkeld was opened in 1809. The technical knowedge applied by Telford finally enabled such a bridge to be successfully constructed at this point. It proved to be an important factor in the modernisation of communications between the Highlands and the Lowlands.

him play and many famous visitors were brought to the inn by the Duke. Gow died in 1807 and his epitaph read:

> Gow and Time are even now.
> Gow beat Time, now Time beats Gow.

Gow is buried in the churchyard at Little Dunkeld where his tombstone still stands. The cottage where he was born and later lived can be seen in the village of Inver.

The Dunkeld ferries mostly plied across a smooth passage, but in spring and autumn great spates flooded downstream, making the water difficult and dangerous to cross. The level was known to rise seventeen feet in a short space of time and the skilled ferrymen harnessed the strength of the current to help to manoeuvre the boat from one side to the other. In

1766, there was a fatal accident at the East ferry when six out of thirteen passengers perished as the boat hit a boulder and water rushed in. Four horses also being transported jumped overboard and swam ashore. Telford built a toll bridge to replace the ferries and the toll cottage still stands at the south end of the bridge. The resentment of the citizens of Dunkeld against bridge tolls reached such a pitch in 1868 that troops were sent to keep the peace. Bridge tolls had been extracted indiscriminately from local people and strangers alike. Townsfolk had to pay a toll both ways when attending church at Birnam and Little Dunkeld. The arrival of the railway in 1856 meant that passengers living in Dunkeld had to pay a bridge toll before they even reached the station. The unfairness of the position as between those living in Dunkeld and those residing in Birnam and Little Dunkeld flared into animosity. Finally, in 1879, the big, white toll-gate was removed together with the bridge charges and the people of Dunkeld no longer felt exploited.

Of the remaining ferry locations between Dunkeld and Kenmore, Logierait is the most famous. The rivers Tay and Tummel, being in close proximity, form an important meeting place on the great road northwards to Inverness. Robert III built himself a castle at Logierait and the Dukes of Atholl administered justice at the court of Regality held there until 1748. A grand hall seventy feet long, with galleries at either end, described as 'the noblest apartment in Perthshire', accommodated the court. Beside the court house a gaol was built. Rob Roy, once gaoled at Logierait, escaped and avoided the fate of many who were hanged from the huge ash tree, sixty-three feet high and forty feet wide, which stood beside the east ferry landing place. The passage of the ferry was not always easy and Robert Heron, an inveterate traveller in eighteenth-century Scotland, described how the ferryman was obliged to row standing in the stern of the boat like a punter. In 1824, one of James Fraser's twin-hulled boats was put on this passage and was worked by James Stewart for twenty-seven years. His grave can be seen

The gravestone of James Stewart, ferryman at Tummel Ferry for twenty-seven years, can be found in Logierait churchyard. He died in 1873 aged 45 years.

in the churchyard at Logierait near the east ferry landing place. In 1911, the chain-driven ferry boat was still in operation and ran parallel to the handsome iron railway bridge which was constructed in 1888 at a cost of £2,800.

Other ferry locations on the Tay between Logierait and Kenmore were less widely used by the public at large but were important to the local community. In the seventeenth century, the ferries at Pitnacree, Aberfeldy and Kenmore were ideal escape routes for the transportation of stolen cattle. This illegal trade was regular and lucrative until a decree was issued by the Privy Council in 1681 demanding that these boats 'be put under securitie and good caution' in an attempt to control the level of theft. General Wade tried a different method of control in building roads which gave better access to the hinterland. His greatest feat was the erection of a stone bridge, forty feet long with a central arch of sixty feet, at Aberfeldy which was completed in 1731. A couplet of the time extols General Wade's achievements:

If you'd seen these roads before they were made
You'd hold up your hands and bless General Wade.

In the 1890s, the Weem hotel, an old ferry inn situated on the north side of the river, sought to attract Victorian visitors through persuasive advertising. The hotel claimed to offer 'hot, cold and shower baths, a large and handsomely furnished Public Room and suites of Spacious Apartments. The Posting Department comprises open and close Carriages, Wagonettes, Dog Carts etc. of the most modern description, with very superior horse'. There was assurance that 'Every attention is paid to domestic comfort'. Today, Aberfeldy attracts tourists and General Wade's well-constructed bridge withstands the weights of modern traffic and remains a monument to the builder. Most tributaries of the Tay with their rocky beds, fast-flowing waters and narrow passages make crossings difficult. Nevertheless, a few ferry boats did operate at some places. In 1801, such a ferry still existed at Invergarry when John Bristed, an American traveller, wanted to cross during his journeying round Scotland. Bristed was appalled by the 'suffering of the very extremes of poverty and wretchedness' of the ferryman. At first, the ferryman refused to take the 'bawbie' offered by Bristed, being convinced that Bristed and his companion were 'worse off than himself' and he 'scorned to oppress the poor'.

In 1909 trains ran side-by-side with the Logierait ferryboat over the Tay. The winding mechanism for propelling the ferry is placed beside the track leading to the ferry landing stages with the boat moving broadside across the water.

An earlier ferryman, in 1767, was persuaded to attempt to ferry too many passengers when the River Garry was in spate. The overcrowding resulted in the boat capsizing and eighteen people being drowned. A poem, entitled 'Song on the loss of the Boat of Innergarry', written by Alastair Campbell, commemorates the tragedy and graphically describes the search for bodies. These small river ferries did not serve any great national communication route because the most frequented and established highway followed the coastal plain on the east coast of Scotland. The principal obstacles on this route were the North Sea outlets of the rivers Esk, Dee and Don which either had to be circumnavigated or crossed. In 1178, on the River Esk, the

35

right of ferry at the crossing from Ferryden to Montrose was transferred by David II to the new Abbey of St. Thomas at Arbroath. Thereafter, the ferry belonged to the Abbey until the Reformation when it passed into the hands of the lairds of Rossie. Between 1755 and 1758, Archibald Scott of Rossie disputed with Montrose Town Council regarding improvements at the ferry. A compromise was reached and the expenditure was halved between the two protagonists. The ferry continued to operate until 1795 when a handsome toll bridge was built. Scott of Rossie, as proprietor of the ferry, was awarded £2,825 in compensation for the loss of revenue but the ferrymen merely lost their jobs. On the day the bridge was opened the ferrymen marched across the new bridge in single file, each shouldering an oar draped in black crepe. In spite of the existence of the bridge the ferry was resuscitated in the nineteenth century when the lassies, living in Ferryden but employed in Montrose by Patons thread mill, required to cross the river to go to work.

At Aberdeen, the wide mouth of the River Dee created problems of transportation from earliest times. In 1459, proposals to build a bridge at this point were agreed by the burgesses of Aberdeen, and John Livingston, vicar of Inverngy, 'with property in the Castlegate and interested accordingly in the common weal', was designated to superintend the project. However, nothing was accomplished and, for a further sixty years, Aberdonians and travellers had to be content either to ford the Dee or to use the ferries provided at Torry and Ferryhill. Although a bridge was built over the Dee in 1527, the ferry at Torry continued to function until the late nineteenth century. It took a terrible ferry disaster on 5th April 1876 before the Victorian bridge was finally built in 1881. It was a spring holiday in Aberdeen, and although the river was in spate, people crowded onto the ferry. In spite of a new chain-driven ferry boat having been installed, the force of the swollen waters snapped the chain and the boat turned over. Seventy-six people had packed into it and thirty of them drowned. It was not until a week

Lassies living in Ferryden in the 1890s were employed at Paton's thread mill in Montrose and crossed over the Esk to work. The girls had to balance precariously on the rungs of a narrow plank to board the ferryboat.

later that the corpses were found huddled together on the river bed.

In spite of a few fatal accidents on the River Dee, it was generally thought of as a romantic and beautiful river. Byron visited the area between 1795 and 1797 and carried away distinctive memories of the countryside. Poems were penned which eulogised the river and the publication of such verse coloured the public's impression of it. More than twenty ferry locations have been identified on the Dee, all of them dating from ancient times, and at least five of them were still in use in the 1920s. Ferries were essential to those living near the river. Until the end of the eighteenth century, only two bridges spanned the seventy-mile stretch of river; there was the old bridge at Braemar and a second, two miles south of Aberdeen, on the great post road from Edinburgh.

In 1726, unsuccessful attempts were made to raise enough money to build a bridge at Ballater, which was the centre of the parishes of Tulloch, Glen-Gairn and Glen Muick. It was not until 1778 that a bridge was finally erected at a cost at £1,700. Twenty years later this bridge was swept away by floods and ferries were in use until a second bridge was put up by Telford in 1809. This bridge suffered the same fate as its predecessor when, in 1829, it was destroyed by fierce spates. Again, ferry boats were reinstated. By 1834, a four-arched wooden bridge finally replaced the ferry but this was not suitable for the volume of traffic crossing it, especially as wheeled traffic increased greatly as the nineteenth century passed. Consequently, in 1885, a solid granite bridge was erected which survives to this day.

Many ferrymen's houses on the Dee were converted into inns. In peaceful times, these hostelries were frequented by local folk and cattle drovers but in 1745, during the Jacobite uprising, they provided sanctuary for fleeing Jacobites seeking shelter. After the battle of Culloden in 1746, Strathdee was a hotbed of escaping Jacobites and the ferries crossing the river were in constant use. At dead of night, wanted men were transported clandestinely. John Ross, a Jacobite sympathiser, was the ferryman at Waterside of Birse. He was immortalised in a popular Jacobite song:

> Come boat me o'er, come boat me o'er
> Come boat me o'er to Charlie.
> I'll gie John Ross anither bawbee
> To ferry me o'er to Charlie.

The Aboyne ferry, one-and-a-half miles upstream from Waterside of Birse, was still functioning in the nineteenth century, although strong arguments in favour of building a bridge were put forward. Nevertheless, it was one thing to talk and quite another to act. It was only when a ferry boat

Mary Pirie or Sinclair, the ferrywoman at Boat of Fechil, by Ellon, on the Ythan, worked the ferry for forty years while simultaneously managing a croft and bringing up a family.

disaster occurred that the issue was forced. One Fair Day in 1827, when the river was in spate, people thronged to Aboyne. Homeward bound on a dark, wet night, the heavily-laden ferry boat left the north bank to cross the swollen river. It overturned, throwing out all the passengers. A woman and baby drowned while the rest were fortunate to escape with their lives. The survivors landed on the south bank and the ferryman had to trudge via the bridge at Portarch to alert the people in Aboyne. A new bridge, built the following year, succumbed to the terrible floods of 1829 and once again a ferry boat served the community. At his own expense, the Earl of Aboyne erected a suspension bridge. It was described as 'awfu' slim and had an awfu' shak in it. The bairns had a fine time swinging on it'. By 1869, the volume and weight of traffic at Aboyne rendered the suspension bridge useless and ferry boats were re-established. Finally, in 1871, at a cost of £3,000, a third bridge was completed and this proved to be an asset both practically and aesthetically.

The Don, 'twin stream of the Dee', is essentially gentle and calm, possessing little of the impetuousness of the Dee. The Don had few ferry locations, being readily fordable. Monymusk had a ferry site and an inn with a reputation which spread beyond the immediate locality and was highly recommended on the grounds that it was kept by 'persons of respectable character who discourage drinking to excess . . .', which seems rather an unusual recommendation at such a period and in such a locality. In 1890, one proprietor of a ferry on the River Don decided to exert his right of ferry to discomfit those who used the ferry. The previous year, Mr. Garden had purchased the Stoneywood estate which included the right of ferry. Mr. Paton owned the Grantholme estate on the opposite bank of the Don, and until Mr. Garden arrived this ferry had always been a public one. The two owners had been in conflict concerning business dealings in Aberdeen which was compounded when Mr. Garden withdrew hs permission for the ferry boat to use the landing site on his private property. Mr. Paton reacted angrily, accusing Mr. Garden of a 'purely vindictive act . . . taken in retaliation'. Mr. Paton declared, 'I desire to represent to you that the closing of the ferries, while primarily intended to inflict annoyance on myself and my family by obliging us to go a mile further in order to reach the railway, has other consequences of which you are, or should be, aware; 1. It obliges those of your workmen who live on this side of the river to make a long detour in order to reach their work, thus either compelling them to leave their houses or situations or seriously curtailing their already short hours of rest; and 2. It places great, if not insurmountable obstacles in the way of my own servants and other residents in this neighbourhood attending their churches on Sundays. Whatever annoyance you may consider yourself called upon to inflict on me, I still trust that you will not allow your vengeance to fall upon people in humble circumstances who will suffer through no fault of their own'. Mr. Garden ignored these pleas and continued to deny access to the ferry boat. There was little Mr. Paton could do, except to fume!

Again, following the main north route on the eastern seaboard, the next passage to be crossed is the River Ythan. Even in the twentieth century, this river mouth could be navigated as far as Ellon. Further west along the river, two or three ferries provided a service. The Boat of Fechil, an ancient ferry location, was served by a woman between 1909 and 1950. 'Boatie Mary Pirie' was a kenspeckle figure and her son Tom, who succeeded his mother as ferryman at Boat of Fechil, was still ferryman there in 1978 at the age of 84. Tom's description of his mother's lifestyle vividly captures the times in which she lived. As well as 'oaring the boat', she worked the croft and brought up a family. Boatie Mary had a milking cow and a calf and sold milk to workers on the nearby 'Meadows' for 'their dinner pieces'. She even supplied boiled potatoes and made up dinners for some of the men. Tom Pirie tells of the changes in the flow of water and the consequences of that: 'The width of the river expanded from 200 yards in summer to over 300 yards in winter and at a fair run [current]'. He comments, 'My mother was a hard-working woman. When the river was in spate, the coble took a fair bit of hard work, especially when it was dark. At that time, there was only a lantern [on the boat] and if there was a gale blowing, the lantern sometimes went out. Then it was a hit or a miss to get the right place for landing'. Boatie Mary received little remuneration for her efforts. The fare charged was 'Ane old penny' but 'the postman, the packman, the minister, the laird of Ellon castle [he was the proprietor of the ferry], his game-keepers and crofter's wives' were all free of charge. As her son recalls, Mary 'liked all the news' and readily accepted 'the chat' in place of cash. Of course, 'the game-keeper handed over a fish or a rabbit and many a jar of jam came from the wives', so payment was made in kind. Tom concludes his summary of life as a ferryman saying, 'There is still a ferry here and there will be until I am carried away which, I hope, will not be for a long time yet'.

On the post road between Aberdeen and Inverness, five rivers, the Deveron, the Spey, the Findhorn, the Lossie and the Nairn, bar the traveller's way. The courses of these rivers run northwards from sources in the mountains to the Moray Firth. At the mouth of the Deveron, the royal burgh of Banff was a port and a trading centre. Roads from Aberdeen, Turriff, Peterhead, Huntly and Keith met at Banff and a ferry existed there until the late eighteenth century. Over the years the ferrymen were the target for complaints but, in the seventeenth century, they sometimes performed a service which met with the approval of the whole community. For example, on 17th July 1683, the magistrate of Banff 'seriouslie considered how wicked, pernicious and scandalous [was] the life of Beatrix Anderson'. The Council sat in judgement, then ordered that 'the town be purged and freed of such a pestiferous and wicked persone' and ordained that 'the said Beatrix be conveyed . . . with the hand of the hangman to the ferrieboat and to be putt over to the other syde and thereafter banisht from the town for ever'. A similar punishment was inflicted upon Thomas Mackurachan and Margaret Smith on 5th June 1700 when they were convicted of stealing meal, bread, a plaid etc. They were to be taken by the hangman and 'scourged furth the toune at the ferrie boat and

A September crossing in 1898 over the Spey at Boat-of-Garten using a twin-hulled, chain-driven ferryboat. Queen Victoria set a fashion for holidays in Scotland when she purchased Balmoral, and many Victorians spent their summers in the beautiful Spey valley.

bannished furth the toune, never to be seen therein under paine of death, the man to be hanged, the woman drowned'. There is no record of the fee extracted by the ferryman for carrying out such a service. The ferry at Banff finally ceased in 1779 when a bridge was built at a cost of nearly £10,000 and was said to form a structure 'less ornamental than usefull'. This comment can be assessed today by studying the bridge as it stands.

Following the coast of the Moray Firth, the traveller reaches Speymouth. In 1303, Edward I used the ferry at Boat of Brig on the Spey, where previously a timber bridge was said to have existed, and encamped there. In the seventeenth century, the same ferry and ford were used by Cromwell and

43

his troops. Again, in 1745, during the Jacobite uprising, Sir
Harry Innes of Innes wrote to Ludovic Grant of Grant,
stating that 'special care' must be taken to defend Boat of
Brig. In turn, Ludovic Grant exhorted William Grant of
Burnside 'not to move from these boats but take great care of
them', an order which was ignored when the government
troops marched towards Culloden. The Duke of Cumberland
and his troops crossed the Boat of Brig ferry unmolested
with the only casualty being a soldier who was drowned.

The main post road to Inverness passed through Fochabers,
a poor village until the eighteenth century, situated six
miles inland on the River Spey. The ferry here was known as
Boat of Bog, Boat of Gight or Fochabers. This was a key
crossing on the line of communication from the south to
Elgin, Nairn, Inverness and continuing to Ross, Cromarty,
Sutherland, Caithness and even to Orkney. A number of
ferry boats were established on the crossing which carried a
heavy volume of traffic. The ferry proprietor was the Duke
of Gordon who lived in nearby Gordon Castle. This ferry
was affected by flooding and lazy ferrymen. Complaints
carried some weight because so many influential people
used the ferry. Judges going to the court in Inverness
grumbled that 'the administration of justice was materially
affected . . .', while it was also claimed that 'troops could be
retarded in their march to or from Fort George and from
one side of the country to the other' and that 'the protection
of subjects could be at risk'. A bridge was completed in 1809
by Telford, and although it was partially damaged in the
spate of 1829, it was repaired and remained in use until a
modern bridge was built in the 1970s.

The nature of the river Spey was not always conducive to
the operation of ferries; nevertheless, at least ten small ferries
did ply across the river at appropriate points, and many of
them continued to serve local people until the twentieth
century. Place names such as Black's Boat and Boat of Garten
are often indications of ancient ferry locations. At Black's
Boat, in 1843, Alexander Grant, a carpenter, gained the

Val Bandura, ferryman since 1947, working his ferryboat on the Almond at Cramond in 1988 using a traditional method of propulsion, that is, standing upright and rowing with one long oar from the stern of the boat.

license to ferry from the proprietor, Grant of Ballandalloch. Conditions of the tack included '£7 Sterling of money rent for the Boat house croft and ferry Boats'; and payment to the outgoing tenant for the value of the two ferry boats in addition to leaving two boats 'in like manner' when he gave up the tack. At Boat of Garten, the old ferry was served by an oared boat until the late nineteenth century, when it was replaced by a twin-hulled boat similar to those employed on the Tay and the Clyde. It was not until the twentieth century, when increased numbers of visitors to the area swelled the volume of traffic, that the building of a bridge became essential.

The road to Inverness along the coastline is bisected by the rivers Lossie, Findhorn and Nairn. At one time all these rivers were crossed by ferry but because of the numbers of passengers, the increased wheeled traffic and the lack of alternative routes, bridges were amongst the earliest to be built. However, bridge-building was a slow process and often caused frustration when it came to payment for both materials and labour. In 1629, George Thomson, a master mason, requested authorisation for payment from John, Bishop of Moray, and John Haye, Commissioner of Moray, of the sum of 'the first fyfe hundreth merks monie of tua thousand merkis for building a bridge over the Lossie'. One hundred and twenty-six years later, John Leslie and Will Donaldson petitioned Elgin Town Council to pay them for their trouble in 'purchasing timber, very proper for building such a bridge'. Eventually, the money was forthcoming and a bridge over the Lossie was built.

At Forres, in 1782, thirteen people were drowned when the ferry boat over the Findhorn capsized. This accident resulted in a public outcry but it was not until 1800 that a handsome bridge, consisting of three arches and costing £1,799, was built. In 1829, this bridge was a victim of the terrible floods and once again ferries had to operate. For two years there was dissension between Forres Town Council and Sir William Cunning, the landowner of the proposed ferry location. John Skirving was appointed to supervise the ferry but was forced to resign in 1830 when a new suspension bridge was planned. This bridge, designed by Sir Samuel Brown, was opened in 1831 and superseded the ferry.

Until the late nineteenth and early twentieth centuries, roads north of Inverness were few and poorly surfaced. The

The Cramond ferry tariff in 1988 posted on the South quay. Intending passengers still use the age-old method of attracting the ferryman's attention by shouting for him.

land was pockmarked with bogs, and bridges across them did not exist. There was no urgency to improve matters as the sparse population, little available wealth and few commercial opportunities provided scant incentive for progress. Ferries were not common but boats did provide transport across water passages when there was no alternative. The ferry across the river at Beauly was said to have been in use since the twelfth century when Alexander I crossed there. In May 1646, the Duke of Montrose and his forces used this ferry after raising the siege of Inverness. By the eighteenth century, there were increasing complaints about the unsafe service provided. In 1765, William Mackenzie wrote to the Commissioners of Supply Committee stating, 'My chaise would have gone overboard and the Boat must inevitably have been upset if two of my servants had not been placed at the wheels. In addition, the decay of one of the boats was so

bad that a great quantity of water rushed in, which must
have sunk it but for the shortness of the passage'. To add
insult to injury, the ferryman charged William Mackenzie
2/6d for each crossing. This sum seemed excessive when
compared with the same fare charged to cross the Forth at
the Queensferry Passage, a journey of at least five times the
distance. In 1809, there was a near-fatal accident when the
ferry boat sank while carrying a large number of passengers,
most of whom had been attending church service, but there
were no fatalities. A bridge was hastily constructed and stood
from 1810 to 1892 when it was swept away, and subsequently
a passenger ferry plied the Beauly, with wheeled vehicles
having to make a detour. Accounts of ferry disasters often
portray the resourcefulness of rescuers. The Rev. James Hall
recounted the story of a fellow clergyman involved in a
rescue in 1807. While he was crossing a Morayshire river
with his bride and a servant, the boat, rowed by the minister,
capsized. The cleric and his wife reached the bank safely but
the unconscious servant had to be pulled from the water by
his master who carried him to the nearest cottage. Attempts
at revival included rubbing warm grains of corn all over the
servant's body and using a pair of bellows to blow air into
one nostril while closing the other nostril and mouth.
Although this action was repeated for a long time, the servant
unfortunately failed to recover consciousness.

   The only river ferry in operation at the present time
seems to be the ferry crossing the River Almond at Cramond
on the outskirts of Edinburgh. Cramond village, situated
near the mouth of the Almond, occupies the site of an
important Roman outpost and was connected by a military
way to the English Watling Street and to Antonine's Wall.
The fortunes of the village fluctuated from that time until
the 1690s when two successful iron mills brought prosperity
to Cramond until the 1870s. Throughout the centuries, the
ferry plied the short passage and in its heyday was in constant
demand. Even today, this ferry is much in use. In 1945, the
Earl of Rosebery, the Cramond ferry proprietor, advertised

for a ferryman. A demobbed soldier took the job on a temporary basis, but when he found other work the position was offered to his brother-in-law, Val Badura, an ex-Polish soldier who had been stationed in Scotland. In 1947, Badura took the post which he holds to the present day. During the years, he has seen innumerable changes. In 1947, the ferryman's cottage, situated on the north bank of the Almond, was lit by paraffin lamps and Agnes Badura cooked on a coal-fired range, the coal being ferried by her husband. At the ferry, the fare charged in 1947 was 2d per passenger; nowadays, it is 20p. The ferry tariff board supplies all the details relating to the ferry, just as it has always done. The old, leisurely atmosphere is retained at Cramond with Mr. Badura responding to demand when prospective passengers shout or ring the bell which hangs on the south side. At this ferry many of the benefits and the inconveniences, relevant to all the river ferries in Scotland over the centuries, can still be relived.

This review of river ferries in Scotland over the years highlights the part they played in the communication system of the country before roads were extended and improved, bridges built, railways developed and motorways constructed. An everlasting debt is owed for the service they provided.

CHAPTER 2

Forth Estuary Ferries

Amidst all the major estuaries in Scotland, the Forth estuary holds a prominent place. As one travels from the south, it is the first wide expanse of water to be met on the east coast. Historically, it has acted as a barrier to and a facilitator of communication between different factions in the land. Economically, it has provided a relatively cheap, if often inconvenient, mode of transport and, socially, it has promoted contact between north and south. From the thirteenth and fourteenth centuries, the position of the Forth estuary in the central belt provided a vital link between the prosperous Fife coastal ports of Dysart, Kirkcaldy and Burntisland and the larger seaports of Leith, Granton and Newhaven as these developed in keeping with the growth of Edinburgh. Later, in the eighteenth and nineteenth centuries, changes in agriculture, the expansion of the coal and textile industries, the growth of population and migration to the towns and cities all contributed to greater use of the ferries across the Forth. By the twentieth century, the rapid increase of motor traffic created ever-increasing problems at ferry crossings. Although the idea of building a bridge was proposed as early as 1758, it took nearly two hundred years before the ultimate solution was found when, in 1964, the Queen opened the Forth Road Bridge.

The most easterly ferry passage across the Firth was between North Berwick, in East Lothian, and Elie, in Fife. The Earls of Fife held the barony of North Berwick as well as possessing land around Elie. The ferry passage was named 'The Earl's Ferry' after Duncan, the fourth earl, who used it frequently to visit his estates on both sides of the Firth. Until the late fourteenth century, pilgrims on their way to worship in the famous churches of St. Andrews gathered in their thousands at North Berwick. Although the population of North Berwick was about 700 at that time, it was not uncommon for 10,000 pilgrims to pass through the town in one year. One of the special badges worn by pilgrims is now displayed in North Berwick Museum. In 1373, Robert II recognised the importance of the town by creating it a royal burgh. Tribute was paid to the status of the ferry by the inclusion of a small sailing boat manned by four oarsmen in the heraldic seal of the town. The ferry boat left North Berwick from the site of the present harbour and sailed across the ten miles of water to Elie, landing on the wide, sandy shores west of the Eil burn where a hospice was built for pilgrims to match the one at North Berwick. At both hospices food and shelter were provided by nuns from the adjoining chapels, the remains of which can be seen today. Elie was also created a royal burgh, and a special clause in that charter decreed that 'refugees fleeing by boat from Elie may not be pursued until they are half-way across'.

By 1587, the pilgrims had long departed, and according to James Melville, Professor of Hebrew at St. Andrews University, the boat had become 'old and dirty', with the ferryman equally degraded. By the late seventeenth century, the ferry had ceased to exist as travellers preferred the shorter, better-equipped ferries further upstream. Early in the twentieth century, ferry services revived with the introduction of steam-powered boats on the Firth providing outings for the prosperous Victorian and Edwardian middle-class families who had taken to spending their holidays in North Berwick. The paddle steamers *Redgauntlet* and *Tantallon Castle* operated a ferry service between Leith, Elie and North Berwick until the outbreak of war in 1914 when the boats were requisitioned by the Navy. Since that time, no ferry boat has sailed over 'The Earl's Ferry'.

Through the centuries, the three most frequented passages across the estuary were those from Kinghorn or Pettycur to Newhaven, Burntisland to Newhaven, and between North

and South Queensferry. Additional ferry services did offer
alternative routes from such locations as Dysart, Kirkcaldy,
Aberdour, Inverkeithing and Charleston to the south shore,
but apart from Kirkcaldy, these sites provided little opposition
to the main contenders for ferry business. Prior to the
fifteenth century, there were two ferry sites at Kinghorn
within a half-mile distance of each other. As there were no
quays, wind and water conditions dictated which of the two
locations ferrymen used. The more westerly of the two sites
was Pettycur, which had a sandy, not rocky beach, making
landing easier. Gradually, over the years, Pettycur became
the premier location, although the management of the ferry
continued to be vested in the hands of the Kinghorn
magistrates. Here, as at most ancient ferries, proper
regulations were ordained but few were implemented.
Although ferrymen were a law unto themselves until well
into the nineteenth century, good intentions by the management were evident. In 1425, for example, an act was passed
which decreed that ferrymen 'be ready to serve all men', that
they 'raise, nor take more fare of our soverign lieges for
man, horse or goods but as much as is statute . . .' and that
'the ferriers of the kingdom shall tak' fraught but twa
pennies . . .'. The ferrymen appeared to pay little attention
in spite of additional acts passed in 1474 and 1551. Again, in
1600, complaints against the ferrymen were made that such
'skaffis, skeldrykis and zowis' solicited ferry trade, thus
undermining legitimate ferry business on the Forth.

It is not surprising that the poverty-stricken ferrymen of
Kinghorn tried to prise as much money as possible from
their passengers. Between 1623 and 1627, Kinghorn suffered
'grite miserie and povertie'. This was mainly due to the
capture of 'a nombre of thair shippis be the Turkis and
keiping of the company and equippage of the shippis in
miserable slavery and thraldome'. The people had also
suffered because of a 'grite and fearfull storme and tempest
. . . whairby thair harbourie . . . was totallie overthrowne and
brokin downe' and their 'ferrie boit is brokin . . .'. In the

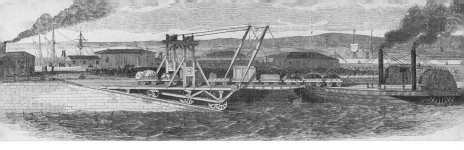

During the latter half of the nineteenth century the *Leviathon* plied between Granton and Burntisland. This 'Floating Railway' was designed to take goods wagons which could be loaded or unloaded.

years that followed, ferrymen from Kinghorn and Pettycur were naturally anxious to re-establish their trade, but as ferrymen at Kirkcaldy were plying additional and illegal boats across the Forth, the business of the legitimate ferrymen was undermined. The ferrymen at Kirkcaldy had previously been restricted to the operation of only four boats but in practise were using many more. Eventually, in 1684, the position was regularised by further legislation which again reduced the number of ferry boats at Kirkcaldy to four, and this proved to be effective for a time. Five ferrymen applied for the four ferry licences. To decide who should hold the permits, David Williamson and Alexander Simpson threw dice, agreeing that 'wha throws most drops shall be preferred'. David Williamson won but his good fortune was short-lived as he was soon found guilty of charging extortionate fares and was punished by his 'ruder and yards' being confiscated and held in custody until he paid the fine.

During the eighteenth century, ferry traffic increased at Pettycur to such an extent that, in 1792, it was decided to build an inn there. £800 was paid to erect the inn and 'sufficient stables and other offices for the accommodation of the passengers crossing at the said ferry'. In spite of this expense, little was done to improve the quays and passengers continued to suffer the danger and inconvenience of having to balance on a narrow gangplank to the water's edge. In 1792, Robert Heron commented feelingly, 'After a tedious passage from Pettycur, prolonged by boisterous wind and the roughness of the sea, I finally landed at Leith'. His fellow passengers included a number of 'Flemish horses of great size' and 'a company of reapers from the Highlands' travelling south in the search for work at harvest time. It was customary for groups of Highlanders to move from place to place, providing labour at harvests throughout the summer months.

In 1817, the dispute regarding the number of ferry boats, which long had simmered between Kinghorn and Kirkcaldy after the legislation passed in 1684, erupted into a full-scale legal battle. Kinghorn brought a prosecution against Kirkcaldy for having at least thirteen ferry boats instead of the stated four. Further statements claimed that, at Kirkcaldy, fares were cheaper but there were no quays and there was little maintenance. Moreover, the service did not include the transportation of horses and carriages and the smaller boats were vulnerable in the face of the strong winds and storms which frequently raged on the passage. Thus, unlike Pettycur, the regularity and reliability of the Kirkcaldy ferries were greatly in question as boats could only operate safely during the summer months or in calm weather. The magistrates of Kinghorn approached the Commissioners of Supply Committee with a petition to appoint Pettycur as the only ferry at that point on the Forth. The decision made in favour of Pettycur was not on grounds of safety, as argued against Kirkcaldy in court, but rested on the precedent that the right of ferry at Pettycur had been established, *inter regalia*, before the fifteenth century, whereas Kirkcaldy could only lay claim to being a free port, a different legal position to holding a right of ferry.

At the Pettycur ferry the number of passengers totalled 36,699 in 1817, but in 1819 that number had increased by three thousand, forcing the Ferry Trustees to consider ways in which to develop the service. It was the dawning of the steamboat age. Kinghorn Town Council turned the situation to a cash advantage by demanding a fee of 150 guineas from the Ferry Trustee Committee for a permit to put a steam ferry boat on the water. The financial position of the Pettycur

An old etching showing two types of ferryboat, one of which is a pinnace in full sail, at the slipway at South Queensferry. Such stone-built quays were only built in the eighteenth century.

ferry remained viable until 1850 when the 'Floating Railway' was put into use at the Burntisland to Granton passage and ferry traffic on the Forth was concentrated at Burntisland and Queensferry. However, steam boats did continue to call at Pettycur until 1939 when the dock was taken over by the American Navy.

Burntisland, less well placed than near neighbour Pettycur and relying on a wider crossing than the Queensferry Passage, had to be content with a smaller ferry trade. The steep hill which had to be negotiated from the ferry landing place also acted as a deterrent to travellers, especially those riding on horseback. In 1591, James VI forbade the ferrymen to transport any passenger to the Lothians unless specifically required to do so by the magistrates of Burntisland, a reference to methods used to restrict the movement of undesirable persons in uncertain times. These measures did not always succeed, and ferrymen were not always willing to be dictated to. For example, in 1615, Sir James Macdonald of Islay, chief of the clan, was imprisoned in Edinburgh Castle. He succeeded in escaping and found his way to the Burntisland ferry boat as it lay at Newhaven. The ferrymen smuggled Sir James aboard and then proceeded to sail round the north of Scotland in their ferry boat until they reached the island of Islay. There, Sir James organised the last Macdonald rebellion but the Burntisland ferrymen were captured and imprisoned for their part in the whole affair.

The Forth estuary was subject to fierce winds and storms, yet, surprisingly few tragedies occurred. However, in 1589, a boat was lost. On board was Lady Jean Kennedy, who had been a maid of honour to Mary, Queen of Scots and who had attended the Queen at the scaffold. Later, Lady Jean married Sir Andrew Melville of Garvock. As she was travelling to Edinburgh to join the court of James VI and Queen Anne, she was too impatient to sit out a storm which was rising when she arrived at Burntisland. She insisted on being ferried across but the ferry boat foundered and she was drowned together with forty others. All the plate and hangings she had intended as gifts for Queen Anne were lost. Charles I was more fortunate, as he survived a stormy crossing but witnessed the sinking of the following boat which went down with all his retinue of servants together with the silver plate and household goods he had been taking to Edinburgh. Many passengers must have clambered ashore, relieved at their survival after the hazards of the passage. In 1648, Sir James Hope of Hopetoun described his experience as 'five hours upon the sea with a varie crosse wind . . .'.

The regulation of ferry fares was always a vexed question, as charges tended to be made according to the individual whim of each ferryman. Crises of national importance such as Cromwell's invasion of Scotland in 1651 permitted such license to proceed unchecked. At that time the Burntisland ferrymen were taking full advantage of the situation. However, during 1651 Cromwell was unable to capture Burntisland and was forced to negotiate a contract with the Town Council. The magistrates agreed to allow Cromwell to enter the town and billet his troops on condition that they worked to improve the streets of Burntisland and built quays at the ferry. In a subsequent review of conditions at the ferry the ferrymen were found to be guilty of extracting extortionate fares, and further legislation was passed to control them. The Deputy Governor of Leith, Lieutenant Colonel Wilks, decreed that, 'It is ordered to be published by the beat of a drum that no Boatman or ferryman whatsoever . . . should demand any more than twelve pence for a horse and man and four pence for a single passenger upon pain of forfeiting 5/− for any default'. Yet only a few years later, Lord Fountainhall recorded that 'For my fraught to Bruntisland . . . 8d', which was double the regulated rate. It appears that the ferrymen were continuing to ignore regulations.

Ferry boats were required to sail in all weathers and under all conditions so they had to be sturdy and well maintained. An account, dated 1690, lists the materials used to repair *The Mayflower*, one of the Burntisland ferry boats. The repairs were carried out by Charles Watsone, James Wilson, James Towrpie and Walter Colier, carpenters. They attested that 'they did really repair the damage sustained . . .'. Their materials included '3 trees costing £10−10/−; half a barrel of pitch at £7; 180 tree nails at 11/−; a barker and a knee head at £5; Two double trees or 12 elms at £2−8/−' and 'For the loss of time until the boat was repaired, £12'. The bill, including other items, totalled £89−11/− Scots and it took three months to complete the work.

In 1790, there were 'three large, stout boats and one small boat' at Burntisland manning the passage to Newhaven but the regularity of the service depended on the state of the tide. Cromwell's quays had long disintegrated as little money had been spent on trying to maintain them. Therefore, landing from the boats reverted to being a hazardous business. In the Statistical Account, the Rev. James Wemyss recorded his hope that 'the gentlemen of the county' would subsidise the building of new piers at Burntisland 'in order to secure a passage for travellers at any time of the tide'. In 1792, Justices of the Peace and Commissioners of Supply for Fife and Edinburgh, with responsibility for overseeing the

Forth estuary ferries, realised that action was essential. New regulations were passed with collectors of fares introduced and £600 allocated for the erection of a new pier at Burntisland. A light was fixed to the pier end to guide ferry boats and £25 was provided for its maintenance. Furthermore, £1,000 was to be spent on building a new pier at Newhaven. The autonomy of the ferrymen was being eroded and by 1814, it was reported that the Burntisland passage boats 'are well mannered and give a ready service'. The increase in ferry traffic opened the way for opportunists and in 1812, another ferry was set up about half-a-mile west of Burntisland. The Starleyburn ferry made a fierce challenge for the passenger trade. It was said that passengers were 'Waylaid and enticed' to use that ferry in preference to the one at Burntisland. An interdict upheld the complaint made by Burntisland Town Council which reinforced the Burntisland ferry as the only legal ferry in the area.

In the early nineteenth century, the end of the Napoleonic wars, the onset and consolidation of the agricultural and industrial revolutions, the increase in population and the growth of the cities were all factors which contributed to changes in ferry traffic. In 1820, the idea of establishing a steam-powered ferry boat on the Forth became a reality. It was estimated that double the number of passengers would use the ferry when steam boats were employed. Thus, a total of 180,000 passengers could be anticipated, with 80,000 paying 2/− (cabin) and 100,000 paying 1/6d (steerage) for the crossing. In addition, the total for goods, carriages, horses etc., could rise from an income of £3,600 to £7,200. In 1828, Thomas Telford recommended that Burntisland be made 'the principle [sic] resort for ferry boats' to connect with the new road to Perth which had recently been completed, thus opening up the routes to the Highlands and the North-East. The new Burntisland steam services required, as at other ferries, the appointment of a supervisor, 'active and able', who was appointed to attend all sailings from 6am to 8pm to ensure that the service ran smoothly and efficiently. He was

FERRY BOAT "ROBERT THE BRUCE" ARRIVING AT NORTH QUEENSFERRY. A.844.

The ferryboat *Robert the Bruce*, with the railway bridge in the background, served on the Queensferry passage for over a decade in the 1930s and 1940s. This boat was the first welded ship to be built in Scotland and the 'double-ended' design facilitated a speedier completion of the crossing, thus enabling the ferry service to run every thirty minutes.

rewarded by a 'handsome salary and a house on the spot'. By 1842, a new low-water pier was erected at Burntisland to accommodate the draught necessary for the safe docking of the steam boat. Changes also took place at Granton, the south terminal of the ferry, which had superseded the old-fashioned location at Newhaven. The Duke of Buccleuch and Mr. (later Sir) John Gladstone held financial interests in land at both Burntisland and Granton and they offered to finance the project of updating the ferry facilities. In return they were awarded the exclusive right to the piers and the ferry.

The building of the railways brought new pressures to bear on the ferry services. The inconvenience and delays at the ferries were seen to be even greater in comparison with the relative speed and ease of travel on a train. There was

increasing disquiet concerning the time lag, additional
expense and the frustration experienced whenever passengers
and goods had to be transferred from train to ferry. On the
Forth, the problem was ingeniously solved by Thomas Bouch
who later masterminded the building of the ill-fated Tay
railway bridge. He proposed a 'Floating Railway' whereby
railway wagons could run aboard a specially built ferry boat
to carry them across the water. The wagons would then run
off the ferry boat directly on to the railway system. In 1850, a
successful trial was held with the boat moving from Granton
to Burntisland and the idea was accepted as practical. As a
result, the *Leviathon* was built. This 'Floating Railway' was
specially constructed to carry between thirty and forty goods
wagons which could be loaded or discharged in about five
minutes. It made four or five double journeys daily. At the
same time, other steam boats continued to convey passengers
according to a regular ferry timetable.

In 1890, the opening of the Forth railway bridge
immediately undermined the effectiveness of the *Leviathon*
but the financial loss was not sufficient to warrant a closure
of the ferry services. Only the demands of the 1914-1918 war
changed the position of ferries on the Forth. In 1917, the
William Muir, the main boat plying between Burntisland and
Granton, was requisitioned for minesweeping duties. However, this boat was restored to the Forth in 1919 and sailed
there until replaced by *The Snowdrop* in 1939, only a few
months before the outbreak of war. No ferry operated on the
Burntisland passage during the Second World War. The
demise of this ancient ferry was legally sealed in 1946 when
the London and North Eastern Railway Provisional Order
Confirmation Act stated that there was no longer any
'obligation to run this service'.

Until the eleventh century, the Forth was known as the
'Scots Water' and the early name for the Queensferry Passage
was Ardchinnechenam. During her reign, Queen Margaret,
wife of Malcolm III, frequently visited Dunfermline and so
became very familiar with this crossing over the Forth. The

association of the Queen with the passage led to its being later re-named the 'Queensferry Passage'. There seems to be evidence to suggest that the name did not exist in 1130 when David I granted 'the ship and passage of Inverkeithing' (not Queensferry) to the Abbot of Dunfermline Abbey. It was in 1164 that the name 'Queen's Port of Ferry' is first mentioned in the records. Malcolm IV granted the Abbot and monks of Scone 'a free passage at all times' over 'the Queen's Port or Ferry'. The previous name of 'Ardchinnechenam' fell into disuse and in 1184, the name of 'Queensferry' was confirmed in a bull issued by Pope Lucius III, Queen Margaret was canonised about 1250 and this added greater status and publicity to the Queensferry Passage. A form of management of the ferry boats began in 1275 when Abbot Ralph of Dunfermline Abbey established '8 oars in the new passage boat'. In fact, only seven persons were allocated oars, with John Armiger holding two of them. These persons, including two women, were 'required to pay 8d yearly for each oar' and to 'perform the usual services'.

Over the years, the Queensferry Passage was patronised by royalty, whether alive or dead. In this connection, sometimes strange happenings took place. When Queen Margaret died in Edinburgh Castle in 1193, the castle was under siege by the usurper, Donald Bane. Queen Margaret's body had to be smuggled out for burial at Dunfermline. All the way to South Queensferry and while crossing the Forth, a mist enveloped the party protecting them from capture until they arrived safely in Dunfermline where the Queen was finally buried. Her tomb can be visited today at Dunfermline Abbey. In 1153, David I also died in Edinburgh Castle and so had to be carried to Dunfermline for burial. When the cortège reached South Queensferry, 'the sea was so boisterous and agitated that they were afraid to venture upon it'. However, as soon as the corpse was placed in the boat, the storm abated and the opposite shore was reached without difficulty, but when the body was taken ashore, the storm broke out again with renewed fury.

Weather was not a major consideration in 1651, before the battle of Inverkeithing, when Cromwell crossed the Forth with 10,000 men although he was 'much impeded for want of boats'. No record appears to be available to show how much was paid to the ferrymen, if anything, for the transportation of so many troops. Four years earlier, Jean Moubray, ferry licensee, was paid the paltry sum of £205 Scots for ferrying 1,000 horses and riders and 1,100 foot soldiers.

In 1842, Queen Victoria and Prince Albert sailed across the Queensferry Passage and were much impressed by the efficiency of the service. On 4th September 1964, Queen Elizabeth, Victoria's great-great-granddaughter, became the last monarch to make the crossing when she boarded the *Queen Margaret*, after she had declared the new Forth Road Bridge open.

Throughout its history, the financial state of the ferry was always of great concern to the current proprietors but financial viability was not always easy to achieve. In 1565 and 1566, Henry Pitcairn, the commendator of Dunfermline Abbey, introduced a scheme which broke new ground in financial dealings at that time. He offered for sale sixteen shares in the ferry. These were so quickly purchased that he added two extra shares, making a total of eighteen sixteenth shares. By 1661, the division of these shares had doubled and there were thirty-two shareholders, who came from different backgrounds. Robert Marshall was 'a ship master, burgess of Queensferrie', while Sir Archibald Primois of Chesters also held shares, but any expectations of great financial return were not fulfilled as, it was reported, 'the ferry business yields a very moderate gain'.

In the mid-seventeenth century, local fairs were popular and the Ferry Fair at North Queensferry on the second Friday in August attracted people from near and far. The central figure at this fair was 'The Burryman'. An exhibition of the Burryman can be seen in the museum at South Queensferry. The Burryman was represented by a youth dressed in wool, covered with burrs from the burdock plant, wearing a crown of flowers on his head, and holding two long sticks decorated with flowers. It was thought that evil spirits were like burrs so, if the Burryman was chased out of the town he would take all the evil spirits with him. The Burryman was also seen as a good luck symbol for fishermen to ensure large catches of fish so, on both counts, the people of North Queensferry held their Burryman in high regard. At the Ferry Fair, the fishermen pooled their catches and shared out the money they received. The idea of groups of workers sharing income for their mutual benefit was not uncommon but it was astute legislation which capitalised on the practice. In 1647, the Privy Council decreed that every ferryman must extract a stated sum from each fare received and put it into a collecting box. This money, known as 'the Ferry Silver', was to be used to finance the repair of the landing quays at the discretion of the Privy Council. At that time, charges for the ferry included 36/— Scots for 'the best boat'; 18/— Scots for 'the lesser boat'; 12/— Scots for a yawl; 3/— Scots for a horse and man and 1/— for a 'footman'.

As the eighteenth century progressed, mounting concern was expressed regarding the dangerous state of the landing places on both sides of the crossing. In addition, there was no regulated timetable, the boats were stationed at the north side, the ferrymen were insubordinate and there was little evidence of any control of the service. In 1749, a review of the situation by the court of the Admiralty at Dunfermline nominated four boats and four yawls to serve the passage and these were to be examined twice every year by 'an able carpenter and sailor'. A bell was to be rung every two hours, timed by the public clock in North Queensferry, and the ferry boat was to be dispatched, whether there were passengers aboard or not. The bell ringer and the clock keeper were each to be paid one crown per quarter for their work. The exception to the tolling of the bell was to be on market days when 'horses, nolt or sheep have to be carried over', and then the boatman 'shall have no regard to the ringing of the bell but shall immediately cross with the cargo'. Furthermore, a master was to be appointed for each ship with responsibilities for the behaviour of his crew and the safety of his passengers. Each night a sailor was to be nominated to be on watch so that if a fire was lit on the south side a boat could immediately be put on the water. These regulations went a long way towards improving the service.

In spite of the tightening of the regulations, complaints continued until the beginning of the nineteenth century when an inquiry into the whole system of communications in Scotland was set up. In 1809, a Forth Ferry Trustee Committee was established. This Committee had powers to implement proposals designed to improve all aspects of the Queensferry ferry service. John Rennie, a distinguished engineer, submitted an estimate of £28,870 for the cost of all the improvements included in his survey. The repairs and new buildings were carried out at a final cost of £33,825, thus providing the necessary facilities for putting a steam ferry boat on the passage. In 1821, the *Queen Margaret* was purchased for £2,369 but the institution of a steam ferry boat did not immediately replace all the remaining boats and the service provided by the steamer was supplemented by four large sailing boats, three pinnaces and three yawls. In addition, the *Queen Margaret* could tow barges while being fully loaded herself. Over 1,000 cattle a day could be transported from the north shore when great cattle fairs were being held further south. Such a volume of traffic was not easy to handle; the cattle droves blocked access roads and caused long delays at North Queensferry. Passengers finding themselves sharing a ferry boat with a load of cattle did not usually experience a comfortable, trouble-free crossing. In 1828, after seven years of ferry service by steam and sail, the Ferry Trustees had a surplus of £304−11/− but it was not until 1838 that a new, larger steamer, the *William Adam*, was purchased, replacing the *Queen Margaret*. At the same time, the supplementary sailing boats were reduced to two large boats and two pinnaces.

In the nineteenth century, the coming of the railways

revolutionised travel, and the opening of the Forth Railway Bridge immediately affected the traffic hitherto dealt with by the ferries. The North British Railway Company were quick to see the advantages of being in control of the ferry service. In 1867, they purchased the rights of ferry at the Queensferry Passage and soon put three steam boats into use. However, over the years, into the twentieth century, the ownership of the ferries did change hands with Messrs. David Wilson & Son, Bo'ness, the Leith Salvage and Towage Company, the North British Railway Company (for the second time) and, finally, William Denny of Dumbarton becoming successive proprietors. By 1934, another *Queen Margaret* became the first diesel-electric paddle-driven boat to be commissioned and, together with the *Robert the Bruce*, the first welded ship to be built in Scotland, served on the Passage for the next decade and more. Both boats were 'double-ended', with an open deck and side loading. The facilities provided by these boats enabled a reliable, regular half-hour service to be kept. Only exceptional loads such as steam-rollers and elephants seemed to pose any problems. Regarding fares, the uncertainty concerning the rate to be stipulated for the transport of a coffin, whether full or empty, was resolved by establishing the fare for a hearse at 10/−, with the driver being charged an extra 7d and 12/6d being paid for a corpse.

In 1949, another new boat, *Mary, Queen of Scots*, was bought and in 1956, in response to the greatly increased road traffic, the *Sir William Wallace* was commissioned. The use of these vessels, together with the *Queen Margaret*, reduced the time taken to cross the passage to fifteen minutes. In winter, however, when one boat was taken out of service for maintenance, the crossing took twenty minutes. In 1962, over one and a quarter million passengers were being transported, together with 600,000 cars and 200,000 commercial vehicles. Cars were charged according to their horsepower at prices ranging from 4/6d to 8/3d. In 1987, the road bridge toll of 40p per car, irrespective of horse-power, compares

favourably with the charge made twenty-four years previously on the ferry boats, although it is questionable whether
or not a toll should be charged at all to cross the Forth Road
Bridge.

Following the advent of steam, the improvement in the
design and performance of the ferry boats was continuous,
but it is interesting to note that it was not until 1962 that they
could be fully controlled with regard to the direction in
which they sailed. Previously, strong winds and fierce tides
had always presented problems to ferry boats and had even
forced the earlier steam-powered ferry boats to engineer the
crossing in a crab-like manner. This method of navigation
was dangerous to other shipping, so, in order to give due
warning to approaching ships, it was mandatory for ferry
boats to have three black balls permanently fixed to the
signal lanyard signalling, 'Keep clear, I am out of control'.
In 1964, the ferry boats were made redundant by the opening
of the Forth Road Bridge. The plaque placed at the north
end of the bridge summarises the demise of the ferries,
stating, 'The Queensferry passage was thus superseded after
800 years of continuous use'.

The need to cross the Forth estuary in its upper reaches
was met by the location of a number of smaller, but none the
less important, ferries such as Aberdour to South Queensferry,
Charlestown to Bo'ness, Alloa to South Alloa and Cambuskenneth to Stirling. Although the ferry passage between
Charlestown and Bo'ness had functioned throughout the
centuries, it had never carried a great volume of traffic until
the middle of the nineteenth century. In 1834, there was a
sudden escalation of ferry passengers at this crossing when a
new pier facilitated the docking of the steam ferry boats.
Hitherto, the design of the steam boats had prevented them
from drawing into the shore; therefore, with no pier at
Charlestown, they had to anchor some way out, and
passengers had to be rowed in small rowing boats from the
steamers to the shore. The new pier meant that passengers
could now walk directly on and off the steam boats. This

To the right the Forth Railway Bridge, and to the left the Forth Road Bridge, still under construction. In the foreground the ferry *Sir William Wallace* is taking cars on board. The year is 1962, and the days of the ferry are numbered.

easier and quicker mode of transport attracted increasing numbers of people. More importantly still, in 1852, a railway line was constructed between Charlestown and Dunfermline which provided the citizens of Dunfermline, and the surrounding hinterland, with a direct route to Edinburgh via the Charlestown to Bo'ness crossing. At that time, this railway was the only line which terminated at a ferry location in the vicinity of Dunfermline. It continued to keep the monopoly of ferry traffic at Charlestown until the railway to North Queensferry was built in 1877, together with a station which was conveniently erected at the head of the pier. After that, the Charlestown to Bo'ness ferry ceased to operate and all the ferry trade was again restored to the Queensferry Passage after over twenty-five years in the doldrums.

There was often a strong link between the establishment of religious centres in Scotland and the development of ferries. From the tenth century, Alloa was a familiar resting place for pilgrims en route to the religious houses in the east and north. The ferry at Alloa was first mentioned in a charter dated 1363 in which David II granted 'his beloved and faithful confederate, Sir Robert de Erskyne', the 'land of Ferrytoun' and other estates. Thereafter, the earls of Mar possessed the rights of this ferry and let out the tack to men such as William Murray of Keillar, Thomas Dawling and John Spence of Blair, who, in 1659, paid '13,450 merks of principal and 675 merks of sheriff fee' for the tack. In 1664, Alexander Milne, a merchant burgess from Linlithgow, took the tack of the grounds of Little Dovan, Langkerse, Powhouse and the 'Pow of Alloway'. This included the rights to hold weekly markets and annual fairs and to rent the 'harbour or shore of Alloway anchorage and the ferry boats on the water of Forth on both sides . . .'. In undertaking such a venture, Milne must have been convinced he could receive some profitable return from his investment which seems to indicate that the ferry at Alloa was, at that time at least, financially viable and therefore well-used.

In the eighteenth century, the Rev. James Frame, in the Statistical Account, called the ferry 'Craig Ward' or the 'King's Ferry', by which time 'very complete piers' had been built on each side of the river. In Alloa, at the beginning of the nineteenth century, the coal industry expanded, the manufacture of glass developed, and great droves of cattle descended from the north and west, so the half-a-mile water passage across the Forth presented an increasingly frustrating obstacle. Complaints were made that 'People who go thither with carts have often to wait for hours before they get a loading'. In 1822, the comparative merits and demerits of building a bridge or buying a steam ferry boat were discussed. It was agreed that 'the Alloa ferry will become the principal point of communication between north and south Scotland' and that a steam ferry boat would be preferable to meet the demands arising from such a position. Consequently, a steam boat was purchased at a cost of £1,400 and a further £1,000 was spent on modernising the piers. These costs were met by thirty subscribers each providing £100. An indication of the returns made from the ferry fares can be seen from the prices charged: drovers had to pay 4d per beast or 5/— per score. In 1823, as profits were good, a second boat was deemed necessary and the subscribers were asked to pay a further 34 guineas each. In 1827, the annual rent from the ferry tack was £500.

In the 1830s, the ferry was taken over by the Caledonian Railway Company who carried out no improvements. In fact, the ferry was neglected and the volume of traffic dwindled to such an extent that the only boat left on the passage was a small rowing boat. In 1869, the Earl of Mar and Kellie raised the matter with the railway company and in the following year a small, double-bowed paddler, the *Countess of Kellie*, was put into use, but it was reported that the 'boat and pier are ill adapted to each other'. Even so, this boat continued to give service until 1886 when the Alloa Railway Bridge was built and the railway company gave up its holding in the ferry. Then Alexander McLeod took over the tack and operated a small motor launch, the *Lord Erskine*, which, when traffic was heavy, towed a barge.

In 1905, Alloa saw the growth of the local sawmill industry and employees required daily transport from one side of the Forth to the other. The demand for a larger ferry boat was met by the purchase of *The Hope*. This boat was fitted with a bell which could be tolled to signal her presence in fog. The women workers at the Alloa glass works also used *The Hope* and often sang:

> McLeod's got a ferry,
> The ferry's got a bell
> And every time the fog comes down
> Sailor rings his bell.

During the 1914-1918 war, the Alloa ferry, and with the Queensferry service, were the only two civilian steam ferries left on the Forth. In 1936, the construction of the Kincardine Bridge undermined the need for a ferry at Alloa and, with the outbreak of war in 1939, the ferry was closed for good.

In some instances in Scotland, the communication between a particular royal castle and a religious institution depended upon the effective functioning of a ferry. The ferry at Cambuskenneth is a case in point. This served as a link between Stirling Castle on the south bank of the Forth and Cambuskenneth Abbey on the opposite side. Cambuskenneth Abbey was also known as 'The Monastery of Stirling' and 'St. Mary of Stirling'. Stirling still has a street named St. Mary's Wynd. David I probably founded the Abbey in 1147, and since that time records refer to the connection between the early Scottish kings and the Abbey. Indeed, in the fourteenth century, the Abbey was an important centre in relation to the politics of the time. In the fifteenth century, James III had a great affection for Cambuskenneth and when his queen, Margaret of Denmark, died, he had her buried there. James himself was assassinated at Sauchie, near Falkirk, and was laid to rest beside his Queen in 1588. A memorial to James III and Margaret was erected by Queen Victoria in 1865 and can be seen at the Abbey today. Cambuskenneth was the centre of great religious festivals and fairs and the ferry was well used on all these occasions with people sometimes overcrowding the boat. Accidents were few, but in 1529 more than fifty people were drowned when the ferry boat capsized as it crossed the short passage of water.

Prolific orchards of apple and pear trees grew in the fertile soil surrounding the Abbey and lush crops of strawberries were so plentiful that a traditional Strawberry Fair was held annually on the 14th of July. On that day, people flocked across to Cambuskenneth on the ferry boat. The advent of the railways brought people from as far afield as Glasgow, and early in the twentieth century the ferryman was able to earn as much as £13 on one Fair day. At that time, the boat was bowed at each end and was rowed by two men operating a single pair of wooden oars, each measuring 8 feet x 20 feet, on a push-pull system. The boat could hold thirty-six passengers. The force of the tide prevented the ferrymen from following a straight course across the water and at night, in the dark, it was necessary to have oil lamps, supported on a pole, at the ends of the boat. Another light was always placed in the window of the ferryman's house in Cambuskenneth to provide a fixed point to enable the ferrymen to navigate safely.

The ferry house served not only as an inn but also as a croft. In the early twentieth century, the Dow family, father and sons, were the ferrymen. The house then consisted of a parlour where the public were given hospitality, a living room, a kitchen, scullery and three bedrooms. Outside, a byre was built onto the gable end of the cottage; there was a boiler house, a piggery for three or four pigs, and hens roosted everywhere. A post box was contained in the side of the house and the postman called daily. After the end of the 1914-1918 war, rope works, a cooperage and a coal mine opened in Cambuskenneth, bringing business and new life to the community while increasing the traffic at the ferry. The appealing setting of the village and the beauty of the surrounding countryside attracted artists and painters. Joseph Denovan Adam set up a studio in Cambuskenneth and taught such artists as Edith Holden, now famous for her nature sketches in *The Country Diary of an Edwardian Lady*. The ferry was a thriving and lively business and in 1919, new regulations were introduced to improve the service. It was stated that the ferrymen must be in attendance from 5am until 10pm; a charge of 1s was to be made for each passenger, exceptions being the village school mistress and her assistant as well as officials of the town. There was an annual rate for the use of the ferry by villagers, and no coal was to be carried. In 1934, a footbridge, which still exists today, was built and the Dow brothers, Thomas and James, the last in the line of so many ferrymen down the years, were able to retire.

The ferries over the Forth estuary formed a vital link in the communication system of Scotland from before the eleventh century until the later decades of the twentieth century. Successive generations of ferrymen gave stalwart service to the communities living in Fife and the Lothians as well as to travellers from all corners of the earth. Now, these ferries are gone for ever, displaced by the need for modern techniques to meet modern demands, and bridges reign supreme across the Forth estuary where once the ferries served.

CHAPTER 3

Clyde Estuary Ferries

The Firth of Clyde encompasses islands, large and small, and sprawls among great fingers of land until it is channelled and narrowed towards the city of Glasgow. Although the Clyde estuary was out of the mainstream of attack from invaders from the south, it did prove vulnerable to attack from the west. The expanse of the Firth served not only to assist raiders but made it easy for them to set up communities with little hindrance. Prior to the tenth century, at least three different factions arrived in the region. From Ireland came the Scots bringing with them the Gaelic language; from Strathclyde, Ninian, a Briton, came to introduce Christianity; and later, the maurauding Vikings and Norsemen plundered and harried the whole area. Only in 1164, after a bloody sea battle on the Clyde near Renfrew, when Somerled, the great Norse leader, was killed, did peaceful integration between the warring groups really begin to take place. The Clyde estuary was also well within the range of the Christian missionaries being sent out from Iona from the seventh century onwards. St. Kentigern or Mungo, one of their number who died in 612 A.D., laid the foundations of Christianity in Strathclyde and eventually became the patron saint of Glasgow. These early immigrants left clear evidence of their journeyings on the Clyde as at least fifteen canoes, made of hollowed tree trunks, have been discovered over the last 300 years in various silted mudbanks between Govan and Bowling.

The growth of Glasgow, elevated from a village to a royal burgh as early as 1175, with a new cathedral built in 1197, stimulated communication with the nearby villages of Govan, Renfrew and Dumbarton and accelerated the need to establish recognised crossings over the Clyde. In 1350, a new stone bridge was erected over the Clyde in the centre of Glasgow; otherwise crossing the water was undertaken either by ferry boat or by fording. In the fourteenth century, the nature of the estuary bed was such that it was safer to ford at a number of places where shoals of sand and gravel accumulated through the drifting of the tide which made the water too shallow for the easy passage of boats. At deeper water crossings, ancient ferry locations were established from Inverkip to Dunoon, Cloch Point to Dunoon, Greenock to Helensburgh, Bowling to Old Kilpatrick, Inchinnan to Dalmuir, Renfrew to Yoker and Govan to Pointhouse. It was not until the seventeenth century that positive action was taken on the Clyde to try to redistribute, widen and deepen the shallow sections of the estuary bed.

Dunoon has a pleasant situation overlooking the Firth of Clyde from the district of Cowal on the opposite shore to the promontory of Cloch Point near the village of Inverkip on the Ayrshire coast. The ferry at Dunoon was its most important asset, with the passage to Cloch five miles distant linking the lands of Argyll and the Western Highlands to the more highly populated and industrial areas round Glasgow and the Strathclyde hinterland. The first record of this ferry, in a sasine dated 1618, refers to 'Alexander Campbell, alias McIver, now of Kilbryde', who was granted the lands of Dunoon, together with the right of ferry, by the Earl of Argyll. By 1658, according to another sasine dated 27th October, Iver Campbell received 'the ferry boat of Dunoon and the lands of Ballochyle and Dunoon' in return for undertaking 'the duty of ferrying'. From that time, Campbell clansmen were installed to serve at this and other ferries in Argyll mainly for the convenience of the Earls of Argyll, their families and servants. The most frequented ferry passage lay between Dunoon and Cloch but a service also operated between Dunoon and Inverkip.

As the eighteenth century progressed, cattle trade from the Western Isles developed and increasing numbers of

West Ferry, Langbank.

The West Ferry inn which included a bar, a bar parlour and two sitting rooms, continued to function in the twentieth century until it was finally demolished in the 1960s.

drovers, traders and beasts used the Dunoon ferry to reach the markets held in Greenock, Gourock and Glasgow. The ferryman enjoyed some social standing in Dunoon, perhaps because of the high quality of food and drink available at the ferry inn. The ferrymen at Cloch were renowned for keeping the best small-still whisky, which attracted many eager buyers. However, much of this whisky was eventually imbibed by the ferrymen themselves as it was common practice for passengers to supplement the ferry fare with a bottle of whisky for the ferryman. Therefore, it is not surprising to learn that the ferryman was often reluctant to launch the ferry boat if he was only going to receive the basic fare of 1/— for the hire of the boat or 3d for each passenger. At both sides of the passage, the boat had to beach on the shore, and by 1767, the volume of traffic was so great that the need for a proper quay had become crucial but nothing was done. Towards the end of the eighteenth century, great droves of cattle arrived at Dunoon to be transported to

Ayrshire and continued to have to scramble aboard the ferry
boats from the shore in a manner that was nothing less than
chaotic. Shipowners, reaping the benefits of the growing
traffic on the Firth, demanded that lights should be erected
to indicate the passage of their ships at night. Consequently,
a lighthouse was constructed at Cloch on 11th August 1797
and manned by a Greenock river pilot, Allan McLean, who
was paid a salary of £30 per annum and allowed to continue
to do duty as a pilot when his obligations as lighthouse
keeper permitted. This lighthouse also provided the ferrymen with a welcome navigation point as it lit up the
approaches to Cloch.

   In 1777, and again in 1813, problems arose between two
Campbells as there was disagreement between Campbell of
Ballochyle and Campbell of Glendaruel which resulted in
arbitration by the Court of Session. In 1777, Campbell of
Ballochyle successfully claimed droving rights for cattle in
transit from the Western Isles and the right to ferry them
from Dunoon. In 1813, the same gentleman protested that
Duncan Campbell of Glendaruel's newly established ferry
plying between the nearby village of Kirn to Cloch, on the
Ayreshire coast, infringed Ballochyle's right of ferry from
Dunoon. Duncan Campbell, proprietor of the ferry at Kirn,
responded by arguing that the crossing from Kirn to Cloch
was three-quarters of a mile shorter than the passage from
Dunoon and that 'in bad weather a boat can get out and pass
from Kirn to the opposite side but not from Dunoon'. This
verbal battle went on for some time but eventually a
compromise was reached on the grounds that Dunoon should
retain its prominent position but Kirn could continue to
operate on such a scale as would make the ferry viable and
satisfactory to the proprietor. After the advent of steam,
when rowing boats at first had to be used to convey steamer
passengers ashore, a pier 130 yards long was built at Dunoon
to enable people, animals and vehicles to land direct, thus
consolidating the status of Dunoon as a ferry terminal for
Clyde steamers.

A view of the Erskine ferry on the Clyde in 1904, including the ferryman's cottage in the foreground. Even then there was no proper access road although this chain-steam-driven ferryboat was the main form of tranport over the Clyde at this point.

In 1820, sixteen steam boats based at Gourock plied on the Firth of Clyde, so the cross-channel route from Dunoon to Cloch was replaced by the longer but busier crossing between Gourock and Dunoon. However, a small ferry boat did continue to serve the Dunoon and Cloch passage for the benefit of passengers only. In the twentieth century, the growth in the number of petrol-driven vehicles demanding to use a ferry from Dunoon to Cloch resulted in several petitions being submitted pleading for the return of a vehicular ferry to run on this route in order to reduce the eighty-mile road journey from Dunoon to Gourock.

In 1948 a statutory enquiry was set up by the Minister of Transport to investigate the position of ferries in Great Britain. Their current function and future potential were considered together with their financial viability. The enquiry findings were seriously considered by the Ministry of Transport. In many cases ferry boats were immediately upgraded to cope with the increasing volume of vehicular traffic and, in the longer term, recommendations to replace certain ferries by bridges have been fulfilled. In the case of Dunoon and Cloch, 'a ferry for vehicles and passengers should be instituted', but this recommendation was never implemented. Suffice to say that forty years later there is still only one ferry which sails between Dunoon and Gourock although it makes sixteen daily journeys between 6.45 and 21.05 and the crossing nowadays takes only twenty minutes.

The Greenock to Helensburgh ferry, in contrast to most other ferries on the Clyde estuary, could not claim to be of great antiquity. The town of Helensburgh originated with the proliferation of building undertaken by Sir James Colquhoun in the late 1770s and the town expanded as a commuter base for wealthy Victorians making their money in Glasgow. In the mid-nineteenth century, the pier at Helensburgh was constructed at some considerable expense to accommodate the steam boats then sailing up and down the Clyde. As a railway terminal, the town continued to attract residents and holidaymakers and, at the beginning of the twentieth century, the railway company put a steamer on a regular ferry service between Greenock and Helensburgh. In 1905, when there were eight daily sailings, passengers travelled free while 1/— per hundredweight was charged for a car. By 1914, cars were only accepted on condition that 'the deck of the ferry boat was level with the pier', a notice of twenty-four hours was given, and the weight of the car was not more than fifteen hundredweight. In 1931, the steamer was undertaking only two sailings daily and the charge for a car was 25/— for fifteen hundredweight, 30/— for twenty-five hundredweight and 35/— for over twenty-five hundred-weight. This service was thought to be inadequate and, in 1948, the ferry review recommended that 'a ferry for vehicles and passengers should be instituted to form a link between Greenock and Helensburgh'. This proposal was never implemented and travellers to Glasgow had to rely on road links.

In 1913, the Erskine Ferry arrived at a gas-lit landing area at Kilpatrick on the north bank of the Clyde. One day in 1935, the usual steady flow of ferry traffic suddenly increased. The Erskine ferry enjoyed the busiest day on record in coping with the multitudes who had flocked to the Clyde to witness the launching of the famous *Queen Mary*.

There was an ancient ferry at the village of Cardross and the passage crossed the Clyde to Port Glasgow. Even in the nineteenth century, the ferry boat remained an open rowing boat and was never replaced by a steam-powered vessel. This led to an increasingly inadequate service which soon failed to be used at all. The next two ferry sites on the Clyde were about twelve miles upriver: the West Ferry from Erskine to Dumbarton, chiefly used for foot passengers, and the East Ferry or Ferry of Erskine, near the village of Kilpatrick, which transported horses and vehicles in addition to foot passengers. In the eighteenth century, the Lords of Blantyre had succeeded the Earls of Mar as proprietors of the Erskine ferry. In 1777, Lord Blantyre complained that the approaches to the ferry quays on both sides of the Clyde were being clogged with silt. This was due to the work being undertaken

by John Golborne, an engineer employed by the town
council of Glasgow to deepen the bed of the Clyde in order
to allow shipping to dock in the heart of the city. Lord
Blantyre demanded that thirty to forty loads of stone be
deposited to re-form the river bed which had been undermined by Golborne's excavations. In 1778, Glasgow Town
Council paid Blantyre the sum of £40 Sterling by way of
compensation and new quays were built at the ferry. The
draining and widening of the Clyde continued and the
noxious material was deposited at the ferry terminals, much
to the disgust of Lord Blantyre. He constantly bombarded
the Town Council with complaints regarding the methods
employed in attempting to improve the water flow on the
Clyde. In 1825, he protested strongly that a proposed erection
of walls and dykes would spoil the view from his home,
Erskine House, which overlooked the Clyde. In response,
the Town Council conceded the point and he subsequently
built a magnificent mansion on nearby ground. Lord
Blantyre had little time to enjoy his new home and improved
view as he was killed in Belgium in 1830. His son, Robert,
the twelfth baron, continued to be as vigilant as his father in
his monitoring of the changes planned by the newly formed
Clyde Navigation Trust. He was awarded £12,500 compensation in 1875 in response to his claims. Legal proceedings
dragged on until the 1890s when the Trustees finally agreed
to purchase the rights of the West and the Erskine ferries. In
1901, Robert, Lord Blantyre, died leaving no heir and, as a
result, in 1910, the estate was broken up, and eventually
Erskine House became a hospital for disabled ex-servicemen.

Robert, Lord Blantyre, had taken a personal interest in
the ferries. This was demonstrated in 1855 when he invited
tenders for a new ferry boat at Erskine, a new boat that was
going to bring him credit. He specified that it must contain
certain modifications including a hull of iron, shuffing boxes,
cocks and valves of brass and seats of 'Yellow Pine'. In 1860,
this magnificent boat was superseded by a steam-powered,
chain-driven ferry boat but only four years later this boat,

During the 1930s and 1940s, the transport of motor vehicles over the Clyde at Renfrew was facilitated by the drive-on, drive-off system. During this period, this ferry was used daily by hundreds of city workers.

incorporating innovative engineering concepts, came to a tragic end on a bleak March day when a strong wind caused the chain to snap, the boat to pivot out of control and finally to sink. After this accident, a new ferry boat was constructed with double chains. Subsequently, all new chain-driven ferry boats were required to have two chains.

In the mid-nineteenth century, the Erskine ferryman was described in the New Statistical Account as an 'excellent and careful tenant'. He was also given credit for managing a 'neat and comfortable inn' which was 'a favourite resort for dinner parties from Glasgow'. This was the most westerly ferry at which carriages and horses could cross the Clyde to reach Dumbartonshire and the Western Highlands and it was always busy. The fares charged were reasonable: 1d for a foot passenger to 2/6d for a four-wheeled chaise with two horses. In contrast, the West ferry was 'ill kept and little used' and in the 1850s, when Lord Blantyre, proprietor of the ferry, was approached by the Glasgow and Greenock Railway Company for the purchase of the ferry, he refused to sell because unacceptable competition would then be created for the Erskine ferry. Consequently, the West ferry service remained poor and underdeveloped. In 1867, Lord Blantyre took out an interdict against Daniel Broadley, described as a 'labourer', who had set up an illegal ferry service on the Clyde near the West ferry in opposition to the legitimate ferrymen, the Paton family, who had been tacksmen of the West ferry for over 160 years. Broadley was found guilty of encroaching on Lord Blantyre's right of ferry and was fined £16.11.2d.

In the twentieth century, the chain steamboat continued to serve on the passage with passengers paying 1d and cars being charged 6d each. In 1948, the ferry boat could hold twelve vehicles. At that time, the review of ferries reported that the traffic at the Erskine ferry was less than that carried before the 1939-1945 war. Nevertheless, recommendations were made to increase the capacity of the ferry boat and to provide a twenty-four hour service. This recommendation was ignored and public demand for an easier crossing was only met in 1974 when the Erskine Bridge was opened and replaced the ferry.

In the fourteenth century, the shallowness of the Clyde, at both Renfrew, on the south bank, and Yoker, on the north side, allowed men and horses to wade across at the point known as the Marlin Ford. At high tide, a floating raft or rough coble was used and gradually, through custom and wont, a proper ferry at Renfrew came into being. In 1614, the right of ferry was included in the charter granted to the town of Renfrew by James VI confirming its status as a royal burgh. In the eighteenth century, the parish of Renfrew was still divided by the waters of the Clyde and some of the town's revenue was derived from the rent payed by the tacksman who undertook the lease of the ferry. In 1725, MacDougall, in his geographical survey of Scotland, told of 'the handsome dyke of hewn stone on both sides of the water for the convenience of passengers' and mentioned the 'very good change house' at the ferry.

In the later years of the eighteenth century, Glasgow developed and expanded with the successful tobacco trade. The state of the Clyde again proved to be a problem as large ships were prevented from docking at Glasgow. Some further action had to be taken to improve the situation. In 1760, the building of a lock and dam at the Marlin ford was proposed and in the same year Alexander Speirs, a prosperous Glasgow tobacco merchant, bought the land of King's Inch in the vicinity of the ferry landing place. The only road to the ferry was through the land of King's Inch and the public continued to use this access as before. Speirs built a magnificent mansion house near the Clyde but he died in 1782, the year the house was completed. Five years later, his son, Archibald Speirs, felt so unhappy about the lack of privacy he and his family had to suffer from the increasing flow of carriages and people passing over his land en route to catch the ferry that he made a proposal to Renfrew Town Council. He suggested that the site of the ferry should be moved half-a-mile to the west, beyond his land, to the side of the Pudzeoch canal. Should the Town Council agree to this proposal, he would, in return, guarantee to erect two new quays, a ferry house, a stable for six horses and a new access road to the ferry. Renfrew Town Council accepted his plans with alacrity, and to prove their goodwill they contributed towards the purchase of a new ferry boat. The Rev. Thomas Burns, in the Statistical Account, commented, 'There is now a most complete ferry boat, built by subscription, purposely for carriages; in which, by means of a rope fixed upon each side of the river and running upon four rollers, two fixed at each end of the boat, one placed in a horizontal direction and the other perpendicular, any carriage, with a pair of horses, can easily be boated and carried over by one man in five minutes'. This new design, 'made in the Dutch manner', was said by Carlisle in his *Topographical Dictionary* to be 'of great utility in conveying lime shells'. It certainly was

innovative at that time and was able to increase the number
of vehicles, people and goods being transported over the
Clyde, thus raising the revenue from the ferry service. In the
mid-nineteenth century, the ferryman, Robert Jameson, not
only operated this large boat alone but also managed a
rowing boat which conveyed passengers to and from the big
steamboats which sailed up and down this part of the Clyde.
Jameson gave free passage to all schoolchildren going to
Renfrew schools, and parishioners attending church services
were also carried without charge.

By the 1860s, great industrial change had taken place in
Renfrew and the surrounding towns and villages. Shipbuilding, engineering works, chemical and dyeing works
created unprecedented employment, and many of the
workers travelled daily on the Renfrew ferry from one side
of the Clyde to the other. In spite of the recommendation
that all steam-powered chain-propelled boats should be fitted
with two chains, nonetheless, in 1868, the first steam-powered
boat was put on this passage propelled by a single chain
which passed over a steam-driven cog. The chain lay on the
river bed and therefore did not obstruct other shipping
passing up and down the estuary. James Elder, who had
taken the Renfrew ferry lease in 1862, was now paid a wage of
24/– per week but he was in no way responsible for an
incident at the ferry similar to the fatal accident at the
Erskine ferry. On this occasion, in December 1876, the single
chain snapped. Fortunately, the boat did not overturn and
no-one was hurt. In 1880 and 1891, two further accidents
occurred when the boat capsized, but again there was no
human loss of life and only two horses were drowned. When
the steam ferry boat was out of action for repairs the passage
was served by rowing boats which must have caused great
delays and frustration.

In 1897, 1912, 1935 and 1952 new ferry boats, designed to
improve the service and accommodate the ever-growing
traffic, were put on the passage at Renfrew. On each occasion
the new boat was received with pleasurable anticipation. The

One of the steam-driven, double-ended small ferryboats which were a common sight on the Clyde in Glasgow in the first half of the twentieth century. Football supporters frequently crossed the Clyde in this manner, and in the 1930s the shipyard derricks formed a dramatic backdrop to the scene.

boat launched in 1935 had a capacity for eighteen cars and 250 people. It boasted windows in the lounges, possessed two upper decks and gave passengers more space than they had ever enjoyed before. 1952 saw the purchase of the first diesel-electric chain ferry. It could hold an additional four cars and had extra room for still more passengers, but by then the heyday of the ferry was waning in keeping with the gradual decline of the surrounding industrial and engineering concerns. For another nineteen years the Erskine ferry continued but in 1971, when the financial loss incurred amounted to £18,000, it was clear that the end was near. In 1974, the opening of the Erskine Bridge created more problems for the ferry and the final blow came in 1983 when the deficit rose to £500,000. In spite of this enormous loss, it was decided that, although the chain ferry would be discontinued, a passenger service would still operate. Therefore, in 1984, on a balmy May night, nostalgia held sway as the old Renfrew ferry boat made its last voyage. A motor launch, *The Renfrew Rose*, now transports foot passengers and in so doing reverts to meeting demands strangely similar to those which first brought the ferry at Renfrew into being.

The ferry passage, Govan to Pointhouse, located near the confluence of the Kelvin and the Clyde, was once called the 'Meikle Govan ferry'. In 1593, the ferryman, John McNair, was apparently held in great respect. His house, named 'The Ferry Boat', doubled as an inn where McNair sold 'good ale and drove a thriving trade'. However, he became unduly interested in promoting hospitality to the detriment of the ferry service. He was taken to task by the owner of the mill at Partick and accused of failing to find 'sufficient men to serve the ferry'. The complaint was upheld and McNair was duly fined.

In the eighteenth century, the ten years between 1785 and 1795 saw a legal battle concerning the access road to the ferry terminal at Pointhouse on the north side of the Clyde. The conflict began on 19th May 1785 when Robert McLintock, merchant, sent a letter to Glasgow Town Council, in which he intimated his intention to enclose the ground he owned beside the Clyde and in so doing indicated that he would also block the access road to the ferry. In the same year, Dougal McFarlane, proprietor of the Govan ferry, sued the Council regarding the damage done to his ferry quays as a

Picture by ALLAN MILLIGAN

Diesel-powered Clyde ferryboats, numbers 2 and 8, were saved from the breaker's yard in 1981 at a cost of £5 each paid by the Forth and Clyde Canal Society. In their heyday, they daily carried hundreds of Clydeside shipbuilding workers when they were an integral part of Glasgow life.

consequence of the work being carried out by John Golbourne to deepen the bed of the Clyde. Three years later, the Pointhouse ferry proprietor, Claud Lang, made similar claims with the additional request that a new quay be built at the Council's expense. The deiberations of the magistrates ground slowly and it was not until 1791 that the law was invoked by the Council to have the obstruction to the current ferry access road on the north bank removed and thereafter to have a properly constituted road built in its place. No mention was made of compensation for the damage done to the ferry quays at Pointhouse until 1795 when £50 Sterling was allocated to Claud Lang towards the cost of building a replacement quay on condition that the proprietor bore the remainder of the expense. Furthermore, the Council stipulated that the new quay must be of similar design and strength to the new pier at Renfrew. Two years later, no

money at all had been forthcoming in spite of repeated
applications to the Council by Claud Lang, and until he
received the funding he was not prepared to build a new
quay. The stalemate continued and, as the Rev. John Pollock
commented in the Statistical Account, 'the ferry, which is
become private property, has long been in a neglected state'.
The only hope for improvement, according to Mr. Pollock,
was to purchase a boat through public subscription so that
'the inconvenience complained of, it is hoped, will be soon,
in a great measure, if not entirely, removed'.

It was not until 1857, when the Clyde Navigation Trustees
bought the ferry rights of Govan from Gilbert of Yorkhill,
that this ferry came into its own. A large, manually operated,
chain-propelled boat, capable of carrying two carts with
horses, was put on the passage. This type of boat was similar
to that designed by James Fraser of Dowally which graced a
number of ferry passages on the upper reaches of the Tay. In
1875, a double chain ferry, registering about 20 horse power,
was commissioned. This boat, when full, could transport
eight horses and carts, together with 140 passengers, and
worked the passage for twenty-eight years when it was
replaced in 1903. The new vessel was capable of carrying
eight cars, had electric light and was so well suited to meet
the demands of the passage that it stayed at Govan ferry for
thirty-five years. At this time, in 1938, a modern boat fitted
with diesel-electric machinery took its place on the passage,
and on the 18th of September 1940, this boat put into practice
the claim that it could also be used as a firefighting base.
That night, in the midst of a German raid on Clydebank, a
cruiser lying near the ferry was badly hit and blazed from
stem to stern. The ferry boat manoeuvred alongside and the
ferrymen proceeded to extinguish the fire, thus preventing a
disastrous explosion and saving the cruiser. Throughout the
1940s and 1950s, the Govan ferry continued to provide as
good a service as ever but in the 1960s its capacity was
insufficient to carry the ever-growing volume of cars.
Eventually, in 1964, the opening of the Clyde Tunnel

One of the first steampackets on the Clyde near the Renfrew Ferry, with Alexander Speirs' house in the background.

severely reduced the ferry traffic and the boat became under-used. Quickly, the public abandoned the ferry service, the boat was taken off the passage and the ferry ceased.

Two other vehicular ferries were located on the Clyde: the Finnieston to Kinning Park passage, situated a mile south of Govan, and the Linthouse to Whiteinch ferry one-and-a-quarter miles to the north. The Finnieston ferry was a modern one in the sense that it did not function until 1890 and was specifically introduced by the Clyde Navigation Trustees in an attempt to cope with the flood of traffic requiring to cross the Clyde near the centre of Glasgow. The design of the ferry boat was unusual. It could carry eight cars and 300 passengers or a maximum of 700 passengers if no vehicles were loaded. This vessel had the advantage of a platform, controlled by a steam winch, which could be

D

lowered or raised by fourteen feet according to the level of
the quays, irrespective of the state of the tide or the level of
the hull. In addition, the boat was double-ended and did not
require to be turned at each side of the passage as the engine
was fitted with twin driving screws at both the bow and the
stern. This type of boat greatly facilitated the speed with
which crossings could be made and it continued in use until
1977.

In 1891, delighted with the immediate success of the new
boat employed at the Finnieston ferry, the Clyde Navigation
Trustees introduced a similar boat at the Whiteinch ferry.
Dubbed either 'Noah's Ark' or 'Old Nancy', this boat was
continuously in service for forty-six years. Hailed as an
engineering marvel in her day, she was preserved as a model
in the Glasgow Art Galleries in Kelvingrove in 1937. So
great was the volume of traffic over the Clyde in the early
twentieth century that more than 500 horse-drawn buses,
charging 4d per passenger, provided transport from Whiteinch to Glasgow and from Govan to Glasgow. The Clyde
Navigation Trustees, ready to embark on money-making
enterprises, decided to undercut the horse bus services by
offering an alternative, cheaper method of transport through
the provision of small, fast boats criss-crossing the Clyde and
shortening the journeys. Consequently, the services that were
introduced formed such an efficient network of small ferries
that the citizens of Glasgow enjoyed a unique system of
communication and transport which is remembered with
affection to this day.

From the early days of the nineteenth century, passenger
ferries had been employed at York Street, Clyde Street and
Kelvinhaugh. In the twentieth century, the York Street ferry
boat was distinguished by a canvas shelter for the engineer
and the boat was fitted with a plain stove-pipe funnel in
place of the usual black mounted one. At Clyde Street, there
was a fatal accident in November 1864. Twenty-seven men
had packed into the little boat which was halfway across the
water when it was hit by the wash of a passing steamer, the

RMS *Columba*, one of MacBrayne's fleet of Clyde paddle steamers, embodied notable improvements which included large deck saloons and a decorated and panelled dining room capable of accommodating 130 passengers. The crowds aboard indicate the popularity of excursions down the coast from Glasgow.

Inverary Castle. Water cascaded over the broadside of the ferry boat, sending the passengers rushing in panic to the lee side. The ensuing imbalance caused the boat to capsize and nineteen men were drowned. Thereafter, a new steam-driven, double-ended boat was employed. It was steered by water jets and could carry sixty passengers. In the latter years of the nineteenth century, this boat was transporting a daily average of 5,680 people. The boat crossed the passage approximately 270 times per working day of eighteen hours. Crews consisted of a steersman, an engineer and a ticket boy.

In 1888, the Kelvinhaugh ferry had the distinction of being the first ferry to have vertical engines, and in 1980 it was the last small ferry on the Clyde to be closed. Until 1980, two diesel-powered boats, built in 1934 and 1951 respectively, operated twenty-four hours a day, each with a carrying capacity of 140 passengers. Economic changes, which to a great extent dictated the demand for ferry services on the

Clyde, are reflected in the 1980 Strathclyde Region figures. The cost of running the Kelvinhaugh ferry in 1980 came to more than £150,000, with an average of only sixty-seven people making the return journey on a daily basis; a number that priced the return trip at £7 per head.

The historical development of the Clyde estuary ferries gives little indication of a stable pattern, albeit there were periods when a satisfactory and efficient service was being provided and when profit balanced expenditure. Fluctuating demand led to spasmodic interest, variable funding and inconsistent standards. In keeping with their counterparts in the east of Scotland, ferries on the Clyde estuary were essential modes of transport in their day and they faithfully served the public need. There was little public acknowledgement of the skills of the ferrymen who were required to navigate tidal waters, consider ever-changing weather conditions, avoid increasingly large numbers of sailing, and later steam, vessels, adapt to new designs of ferry boat and pay attention to the safety of the passengers. These ferrymen did not hold a high social position in any age but they made an important contribution to the welfare of their fellow men.

CHAPTER 4

Tay Estuary Ferries

The beautiful estuary of the Tay, which is tidal as far as Perth, acts as a natural dividing line between the kingdom of Fife in the south and the fertile counties of Angus and Forfar in the north. There is evidence of prehistoric habitation on the southern shores in the discovery of clay pottery remains and stone arrowheads used by early Neolithic settlers, and near Newburgh a Celtic canoe, made from a hollowed-out tree-trunk, was excavated. Maps of Roman Britain show outposts on both banks of the estuary and a camp at Carpow not far from Perth. Later, the Danes and Norsemen sailed up the estuary to invade lands held by the Picts. All these settlements promoted the establishment of ferry sites on the estuary for various reasons: expansion, trade, defence.

The most easterly of these ferries, Ferry-Port-on-Craig, was situated at a natural point where the crossing is only about a mile and three-quarters. The short passage was attractive to the public in comparison with the somewhat longer passages from the neighbouring and competitive ferries of Sea Myles (Newport) and Woodhaven. Ferry-Port-on-Craig derived its name from the 'craig' or rock used for embarking on and disembarking from ferry boats. It must indeed have been a hazardous business attempting to encourage a horse to clamber aboard a rocking ferry boat from the windswept, slippery, uneven rock surface. It was in 1425 that the first written reference was made to solving this problem when an Act of Parliament decreed that ferry owners would be required to provide 'treene brigges', a kind of wooden platform, for the greater convenience of those using the ferry, particularly for the transportation of horses. During the fifteenth century, James II showed awareness of the strategic importance of this ferry by building a castle on the promontory beside it and, at the same time, erecting a fortalice on the opposite shore, at Broughty Ferry. This is remarkable since it is more usual for the establishment of a ferry to follow the building of a castle rather than to precede it. The erection of the castle at Ferry-Port-on-Craig, together with the presence of an early thirteenth-century chapel, which probably offered hospitality to travellers, indicates that large numbers of people must have used this ferry during that period. It evidently held an important position in the pattern of communication beginning to emerge in Scotland at that time.

In the fifteenth century, in common with the Forth estuary ferrymen, those at Ferry-Port-on-Craig were constantly reminded of their responsibilities in the matter of charging the regulated fares. In 1474, the fare was fixed at 1d for each person and each horse, while a further act, in 1486, stipulated that the fare should be 'ane penie for a foot person and three pennies for a person and his horse', with the threat of having to pay '8/— Scots unforgiven' as the penalty for disobedience. In 1588, the Crown relinquished its control over the ferry and James VI granted 'the lands of South ferry of Portincraig, with the house, port and right of ferry . . . to Sir Robert Melville of Murdocairney' at an annual rent of £25—8—3d Scots. Five years later, a number of townsfolk obtained confirmation of land in their favour from the Archbishop of St. Andrews, and this deed denied the rights held by Sir Robert, who responded by petitioning the Privy Council. For some reason, the claimants failed to submit a defence so the case was awarded to Sir Robert who thus retained his rights.

Between 1568 and 1599, the ferrymen and people of Ferry-Port-on-Craig were unpopular with the Town Council of Dundee. At that period, there was considerable traffic in coal at Ferry-Port-on-Craig with ferry boats being used to transport much of it. Dundee Town Council wanted the coal to be brought to Dundee in order to establish some reciprocal trading but the ferrymen of Ferry-Port-on-Craig found they could make better deals by selling the coal elsewhere and they ignored the demands of the Dundee magistrates. The Dundee baillies were displeased but had to confine themselves to unleashing verbal abuse across the water by accusing the ferrymen at Port-on-Craig of being 'plain enemies of the common weal'. They also ignored various skirmishes that arose from time to time when Dundee traders and Port-on-Craig ferrymen met until, in 1599, the Privy Council required the Provost and Baillies of Dundee 'to find caution that . . . certain inhabitants of the South ferry of Port-on-Craig, sall be harmless and skaythless in their bodies, lands, geir and possessions . . .' or heavy penalties would be inflicted.

During the seventeenth century, the ownership of the rights of Port-on-Craig ferry changed hands on a number of occasions. On 16th May 1737, William Lyon, advocate, sold these rights to the Town Council of Dundee for the paltry sum of twenty-one guineas. The magistrates may have made a good investment at the time but £140 Sterling had to be spent on building 'a new sloping pier' designed to ease the 'boating of horses and other bestial' in 1781. It had taken 356 years to accomplish the construction of a pier suitable for the landing of horses. Even so, this new pier did not altogether replace the old 'treene brigges', as that platform was held in reserve and brought back into use in times of high tide. However, the innovation of the sloping pier came too late to attract enough business to the ferry as the new bridge at Perth, opened in 1772, drew most of the traffic. It was only the continued loyalty of cattle drovers, driving great herds from the north to southern markets, that allowed the ferry to survive at all. The free and easily accessible pasturage for the cattle available on both sides of the ferry acted as an incentive to drovers who also preferred to continue to use their own familiar routes.

Early in the nineteenth century, Telford, Stevenson and other engineers were commissioned to review and report upon the state of communications in Scotland, including the functioning of the ferries. Telford recommended that no improvements should be made at Port-on-Craig; instead efforts should be concentrated on modernising the ferries at Newport and possibly Woodhaven further up the estuary. He anticipated the eventual introduction of steam-powered boats to serve these ferries. Nevertheless, the Dundee Harbour Trustees offered to undertake the expense of building a new pier at Ferry-Port-on-Craig which Stevenson estimated would cost £11,172−8/−. Sadly, there was procrastination and nothing was done. Frustration concerning the poor state of the ferry was evident among the townsfolk until the Laird of Scotscraig, Dr. Robert Dalgleish, took matters into his own hands. He advertised a privately run ferry boat which operated at regular times and charged 4d per passenger. Dalgleish also entered into negotiations with farmers in Fife to establish cut prices for the transportation of their new reaper machines at harvest time at a rate of only 4d for each machine. This enterprise was not viewed favourably by the authorities responsible for the Tay ferries and an enquiry was set up. Dalgleish's ferry was declared to be illegal. Once more the public ferry service dwindled until, by 1845, only a small passenger boat plied across the passage.

In 1846, Ferry-Port-on-Craig became a railway terminal and was quickly transformed into a bustling, thriving community, very different from the somnolent backwater it had become. Significantly, the name of Ferry-Port-on-Craig was changed to the brisker-sounding Tayport. The Scottish Central Railway Company purchased the harbours of the newly named Tayport and Broughty Ferry together with all the rights of ferry at the three major ferries on the Tay estuary. These harbours were at last remodelled to accommodate paddle steam boats. These new steamers were adapted to carry railway wagons in a similar fashion to the 'Floating Railway' at the Burntisland to Granton ferry. The growth of railways in Fife resulted in passengers arriving at

A lithograph of the *Union* launched in 1821, the first steam ferryboat on the Tay which plied between Newport and Dundee.

Tayport by rail ready to be transported across the water to Broughty Ferry. Hotels and lodging houses flourished in Tayport where the population had increased from 920 in 1801 to 2,238 in 1851.

In 1877, the first railway bridge over the Tay was opened and immediately took away all the commercial trade from the ferry at Tayport, but in 1879, it collapsed in the notorious Tay Bridge Disaster and the ferry enjoyed a respite of eight years before a replacement bridge was completed in 1887, again making the ferry superfluous. In 1892, the financial loss at the ferry was so great that the Railway Company tried to close it altogether. Local pressure to continue the service was overwhelming and resulted in the purchase of the paddle steamer *The Dolphin* which was retained until 1920. Thereafter, a privately owned motor launch struggled to continue the ferry service until the changing patterns of life had to be acknowledged and the launch was taken off the water. The final solution to the problem of crossing the Tay with speed

and convenience was to be found in the erection of the Tay
Road Bridge which was opened by the Queen Mother on
18th August 1966. The maintenance of this bridge has posed
continuous problems and a survey carried out in 1988 has
revealed the need to spend considerable sums of money if
the safety of the public is to be ensured.

Sea Myles, later known as Newport, lies upstream from
Ferry-Port-on-Craig, and Dundee is two-and-a-half miles
across the water. In the twelfth century, when the Lascels of
Naughton held the barony of Naughton, incorporating the
rights of 'the Tay ferry' to Dundee, the ferry location was at
Sea Myles. This ferry position was about half-a-mile to the
east of the point at which Newport ultimately stood. In 1481,
Alan Kinnaird granted John Adamson, burgess of Dundee,
'the one half part of his common passage boat for the harbour
of Seamyles on Tay', probably as a settlement for debts.
Throughout the fifteenth and sixteenth centuries, the
Kinnaird family continued to hold the ferry rights for only
half the passage. In 1595, Patrick Kinnaird disapproved of
his predecessor's action and decided to regain control of the
whole ferry passage. He obtained a charter from the Privy
Council granting him 'all haill the passage of water of tay at
Dundee'. However, burgesses of Dundee, i.e. the Town
Council, were reluctant to accept this decree and Kinnaird
was forced to complain bitterly to the Privy Council that
'sindrie of the king's lieges daily trouble, molest and mak
impediment to boats landing at Seamyles'. In 1606, Kinnaird
won the support of the Privy Council, and his position as the
rightful owner of the ferry rights at Sea Myles was reaffirmed.
During this period, the plague was raging in Fife, and in
order to contain the disease all passages across the estuary
were prohibited unless express permission was obtained from
Dundee Town Council. This state of affairs penalised the
ferrymen who, as a consequence of the order, received no
income. It is not surprising, therefore, to find that two
ferrymen tried to evade the regulation, but they were caught
ferrying a woman on a Sunday and brought to trial. They

defended themselves by laying the blame on John Lowson, an influential neighbour of Patrick Kinnaird. The ferrymen claimed that this man had 'boistit' (menaced) them, threatening 'to brek their heads' if they refused to ferry the old woman. John Lowson lived on the south side of the ferry well out of reach of the magistrates of Dundee. The unfortunate ferrymen, being on the spot, were 'apprehended and put in ward'. Patrick Kinnaird, surprisingly, allowed his right of ferry to lapse and in 1641 it was duly transferred when the Duke of Lennox, Admiral of the Kingdom, conferred upon the magistrates of Dundee 'the office of the Admiraltie over the river' with the power to 'call before them all the boatmen and ferriers from both sides of the water of Tay and to fix dues, acts and symbols, as they think expedient'. The ultimate authority of the Dundee Town Council over the ferry was now confirmed.

In 1658, Richard Franck, a traveller who had once served in Cromwell's army, was exploring Scotland and became intrigued by the method of navigation used by the Tay ferrymen. In his book *Northern Memoirs*, he recounted that the stern of the ferry boat was filled with 'little trusses of straw' and described how a ferryman selected a few wisps at a time to trail behind the boat. The direction taken by the straw indicated the strength and flow of the current, thus giving some idea of the course the boat should follow. Such a method of navigation could only operate effectively in reasonably good weather and water conditions. In times of rough seas and high winds the ferrymen had to rely on their own skills and experience to navigate safely or decide whether or not to attempt the passage. Travelling in the seventeenth century was not an easy matter, and a good example of the timescale for journeys was the excursion made by Lord and Lady Grant between Donibristle, near the Forth, and Dundee. In 1663, they set off on a Monday and did not reach Sea Myles until the following Saturday, whereupon it took a full day to transport their goods and entourage across the water between Sea Myles and Dundee.

In 1713, the Guildry of Dundee purchased the lands of
Innerdovat and St. Fort and a new harbour and pier were
constructed close to Sea Myles, thus creating the ferry
location of 'New Port'. However, trade at the new ferry site
did not develop at the expected rate and debts mounted.
The Laird of St. Fort, whose interests lay in developing the
ferry at Woodhaven, saw his way to exploit the situation at
Newport by building a toll road which would give access to
the Woodhaven ferry. In accordance with the Turnpike Act
of 1751, he constructed this road leading from his own estate
at Woodhaven to Cupar, the county town of Fife. This new
highway to Cupar linked with the existing road through Fife
to the ferry over the Forth at Pettycur, thus providing a
more direct route to Edinburgh. As a result, Woodhaven,
not Newport, quickly became the principal ferry on the Tay
to the benefit of the town and the Laird of St. Fort. This
prosperity was short-lived, however, as the bridge over the
Tay at Perth was opened in 1772 and the Woodhaven ferry
could be only too easily bypassed.

Disquiet regarding the state of the Newport ferry at
Newport reached a climax on Sunday, 28th May, 1815, when
a pinnace, *The Ballad Jock*, steered by John Spalding, set off
on an ebb tide with a strong south-east wind blowing and
foundered about half-a-mile from Newport. The twenty-two
passengers were going to a service at Kilmany church
conducted by Thomas Chalmers, the famous preacher. The
loss of life aroused public concern and led to an enquiry.
The following year, William Berry of Tayfield, a wealthy
citizen of Dundee, decided to invest in modernising the
landing place at Newport. No doubt he wanted to emulate
the example of the Laird of St. Fort, the benefactor of
Woodhaven. Berry built new piers at Newport together with
an inn and followed that by constructing a turnpike road
which ran from Newport to Cupar. By that time, the Laird of
St. Fort's toll road between Woodhaven and Cupar had
deteriorated, while at Newport the ever-increasing volume
of wheeled traffic meant that a better, wider road was

welcomed. Competition between the ferries was so great that each ferry more than halved its fares so that passengers could cross the Tay for as little as 4d instead of paying the stipulated 9d.

In 1817, Dundee Town Council scrutinised the ferry accounts and in 1819 were in a position to pass an act which provided a new set of regulations designed to meet changing needs at the ferries. More emphasis was put on higher standards of safety, better maintenance, more considerate behaviour of crews and the regulation of fares. The number of boats was reduced to three large boats and six pinnaces stationed at Dundee and one large boat and two pinnaces at Newport. These were operated by twenty-four 'able boatmen' at a weekly wage of 15/— each. A superintendent was appointed with a salary of £80 per year together with a free house which cost £38—8/— to build. For the first time, tickets were issued to passengers: 'a square shape' to be used when sailing from Dundee and 'a round shape' if travelling from Fife. The coxswain of each boat had to wear a ticket, prominently placed in his hat, with the number of his boat printed clearly upon it. Dogs were to be kept 'in a safe place' and no stallion could be taken on board without the consent of the owners of all the other horses being transported at that time.

The behaviour of the boatmen did not always meet the required standards, although this was no new problem on ferries. In 1820, Thomas Tosh, coxswain of boat number eight, and David Kirkcaldy and Thomas Young, two of the crew, were found guilty of 'secreting part of their boat's freight'. All three were summarily dismissed. This suited the magistrates of Dundee who had no intention of replacing the three dismissed men. Instead, they substituted boys who cost less. Dundee Town Council justified this move by stating that 'It would not only reduce the expense of wages but it would bring up a hardy race of young men for the pass-age . . .'. This long-term optimism was misplaced, as a year later whole boat crews were being dismissed on the acquisition of the steam ferry boat, *The Union*, which was put on the passage in 1821 at a cost of £4,245−8−6d.

In 1823, a second steam boat, this time with reversing engines, was commissioned. This boat, the *George IV*, measured 90 feet by 29 feet and 6 feet 8 inches depth of hold, with two keels, two iron hulls and a single paddle wheel in the middle. Spaces of 39 feet by 27 feet were railed off at either end to accommodate about 90 head of cattle. A rudder was fixed at each end and it was 'a matter of perfect indifference which end of the boat goes foremost, both being alike in all respects'. Carriages and carts could drive on and off without unhitching the horses. Initially, it was proposed that these boats should ply from Dundee to Newport and Woodhaven alternately as both these villages depended equally on ferry trade. Eventually, such was the confusion that only one was nominated, a decision that spelt the death-knell for the other. The influence of William Berry, together with the investment he had made, provided strong grounds for the selection of Newport, and this terminal became the principal ferry on the south side of the Tay while the ferry at Woodhaven fell into disuse. By 1824, the employment of the *George IV*, supported by two pinnaces, attracted a considerable increase in traffic with 100,536 passengers, 474 gigs and 2,564 loaded carts being transported that year. To maintain this public confidence attention was paid to the behaviour of staff. It was laid down that all those employed at the ferries must 'use the utmost civility . . . and that when disappointments or irregularities occur (which it is to be trusted will now be very seldom) they will afford such explanations as the case may require'. In addition, concessions were introduced in 1835 in an attempt to attract even more business. Fares were halved, i.e. 6d per person, if leaving Dundee after 1pm on a Sunday, or after 4pm on other days if returning on the same evening. This enterprise was so successful that it was extended to operate from 3pm on every weekday.

During this early Victorian period, the Newport to Dundee

The *George IV*, commissioned in 1823, was the second steam
ferryboat to serve the Dundee to Newport passage over the Tay. It
can be seen approaching the well-built quay at Dundee to discharge
its cargo.

ferry continued to provide a safe and profitable service. The
possibility of expanding the service by building 'a floating
bridge' across the Tay was mooted. This was to take a similar
form to the Floating Bridge on Torpoint Ferry in Cornwall
and the chain ferries then being put on to a number of rivers
throughout Scotland, but technical and financial difficulties
combined to thwart the idea and the more orthodox ferry
service continued to operate. In 1846, the Scottish Central
Railway Company carried out a 'quiet little transaction' and
acquired the right of ferry which they held until their
amalgamation with the Caledonian Railway Company in
1865. In 1873, the possession of the ferries on the Tay estuary
was transferred to the Dundee Harbour Trust at the discount
price of £20,000. At the same time, the Harbour Trust were
made aware of an ancient but ongoing obligation whereby
Lord Archibald Douglas of Home was to be paid an annual
fee for waiving his right of ferry at Newport and Woodhaven.
It seemed that Lord Archibald inherited the right to levy

certain 'small duties or customs on the Boats plying there
and on the Passengers, Goods and other things conveyed
therein'. In 1873, he was paid an annual sum of £13 – 10/ –
for forfeiting these dues and the Trustees agreed to continue
this payment to him and his successors.

In 1873, the Trust purchased two paddle steamers, each
called *The Fifie*, and these sturdy boats faithfully served on
the Newport to Dundee ferry until after the 1914-1918 war.
Thereafter, the advent of the motor car and the escalation in
the number of goods vehicles and farm machinery to be
transported dictated that bigger and better ferry boats be
employed. Consequently, the *Scotscraig* and the *Abercraig*
were bought. In addition to other passengers, children living
in Newport and Wormit, who had to travel daily to secondary
school in Dundee, used the ferry until a new secondary
school was built on the south bank of the Tay in 1933. It was
only in 1966, with the opening of the Tay Road Bridge, that
the ferry at Newport was superseded.

Woodhaven, the most westerly of the three main ferry
locations on the Tay, had the longest crossing to Dundee.
The great years of the Woodhaven ferry were between 1710
and 1772. The historian, Sibbald, in his *History of Fife*, made
some complimentary comments about the state of the ferry
in 1710. He recorded that the passage 'is well provided with
excellent boats and skilful ferrymen' and that 'the passage
may be made at any time of tide, except at low water in
blowing weather when a large bank in the middle of the frith
greatly obstructs it'. In 1770, the new road built by the laird
of St. Fort from Woodhaven to Cupar promised further
development for the ferry but, in 1772, the opening of the
bridge at Perth dashed such hopes and reduced Woodhaven,
along with Newport and Ferry-Port-on-Craig, to villages
struggling for survival. In 1795, the Statistical Account
reported that 'the harbours at Woodhaven are very inconsiderable'. Furthermore, there was criticism of the ferrymen who
were accused of 'borrowing language and behaviour of those
who frequent the passage, especially of such whom they look

on as their superiors in rank and status. How much it is to be
regretted that from so many of these they often learn to be
rude and profane'. The final blow for Woodhaven came in
1820, when the decision was taken to nominate Newport as
the principal ferry location on the Tay. As a result, a new
harbour, new quays and a new road were built at Newport
while nothing was done at Woodhaven and the ferry boats
there soon ceased to operate. However, in 1869, a boat of a
different kind was put to use in the once-busy harbour at
Woodhaven. A sixty-eight gun, three-decker frigate was
towed into position. This ship, the *Mars*, accommodated 400
juvenile delinquents who were instructed in seamanship and
wood and metal work by a staff of ex-officers and petty
officers of the Royal Navy. The *Mars* was thus occupied until
1931 when reformatory ships went out of fashion, but a
plaque which commemorates 'Our Boys' can be seen at the
old harbour today. The *Mars* was broken up at Inverkeithing
and the Mars Training Ship Fund for assisting young people
was started and is administered by Messrs Mackay, Irons &
Co., Dundee.

From ancient times, at least six ferries operated on the Tay
between Woodhaven and Perth. These included the passages
from Balmerino to Dundee, Lindores to Errol, Newburgh to
Port Allan, Ferryfield to Cairnie Pier or the Heughhead
ferry, Carpow to Inchyra and Easter Rhynd to Kinfauns.
The abbeys of Lindores and Balmerino, built in the twelfth
and thirteenth centuries respectively, together with the
twelfth-century religious centre established at Abernethy,
concentrated communities along the southern banks of the
Tay estuary. These settlements were not a new phenomenon
as the Romans had much earlier encamped in the area and
easy access from the sea had attracted the attention of the
Vikings. Consequently, as the Tay estuary narrowed towards
Perth, crossings became easier and more frequent, though
less important than those nearer the estuary mouth.

In the mid-eighteenth century, the ferry at Balmerino
plied directly to Dundee. The right of ferry was originally

vested in the Abbot of Balmerino Abbey. In 1641, as at Ferry-Port-on-Craig, Newport and Woodhaven, this right was transferred to Dundee Town Council. In 1772, Balmerino also suffered from the erection of the bridge at Perth but even so managed to retain a ferry service. In 1817, it was included in the survey carried out by the engineer, Robert Stevenson. He found that 'large boats can sail only at certain times of the tide and from want of sufficient authority to establish and enforce paper regulations . . . the public are exposed to great danger and suffer inconvenience and loss . . .'. In 1819, an act established a new set of regulations for the main Tay ferries, including Balmerino where new quays were built to accommodate the draught of water required by the steam-powered ferry boat, and it quietly continued to provide a satisfactory service. At the beginning of the twentieth century, pleasure steamers which sailed between Dundee and Perth, calling at various places en route, became so popular that they displaced the ferry service. These pleasure boats called regularly at Balmerino until 1914 when the demands of the war changed the pattern of life and they were put to other use.

The ferry passage from Lindores to Errol was pinpointed in 1748 by Macdougall in his *Geographical Collections* as stretching from 'the pou of Lundores to the pou of Erroll'. The right of this ferry, formerly held by the abbots of Lindores Abbey, passed to Sir Alexander Anstruther of Newark in 1722. At that time, the volume of ferry traffic was sufficient to warrant the use of four ferry boats, two stationed at each side of the passage, but the expansion of the nearby market town of Newburgh boosted the traffic at the Newburgh to Port Allan ferry and contributed to the ultimate closure of the ferry at Lindores. By 1814, the necessary repairs required at the landing place at Newburgh and the quays at Port Allan were postponed while the idea of erecting a pier and harbour about three-quarters of a mile downriver towards Errol was explored. These plans never materialised and instead the quays were repaired and the Newburgh ferry

The *Scotscraig* at Dundee in 1951

continued to operate satisfactorily until 1914 when the regular boat was removed from the passage. Thereafter, a small rowing boat was kept in readiness for the convenience of anyone who wished to be taken across.

Three miles upstream from Newburgh and a mile east of the village of Abernethie, another ferry crossed the Tay from Ferryfield, in the estate of Carpow, to a landing place called Cairney Pier in the grounds of Pitfour Castle. Locally, this ferry was known as the Heughhead ferry. The ferry boats here were capable of transporting both horses and passengers. At Cairnie Pier, on the north bank, a 'well conducted' inn existed which must have provided sustenance to travellers who had to await the ferryman's pleasure. From the seventeenth century, the ferry served a busy commercial community and successfully vied for trade with neighbouring ferry services. In 1845, the right of ferry was held by Sir John Richardson of Pitfour, who modernised the quay to accommodate the new steam-powered boats. This ferry was still providing a service in the twentieth century but, like the rest, it became outdated and was bypassed in the age of the motor car.

In their day, the cluster of ferries confined within the limited geographical area between Newburgh and Perth provided options for would-be travellers requiring to cross the Tay. Remarkably few accidents are recorded, but in the mid-eighteenth century there was a tragedy on the passage between Easter Rhynd and Kinfauns. The ferry boat, crowded with those going to attend a church service at Easter Rhynd, was overturned and all aboard were drowned.

At Carpow, the ferry was situated on the east bank of the mouth of the River Earn where it joins the Tay. The passage terminated at Inchyra on the opposite side and was probably one of the most frequented ferries in the area. In 1647, the right of ferry of the Inchyra to Carpow passage was vested in Andrew Blair, brother of Sir Alexander Blair of Balthayock, and furthermore, in 1662, the lands of Inchyra were created 'an whole and free barony' in favour of the said Andrew Blair. He erected toll bars at the entrance to the village of Inchyra where the toll could be paid in kind as well as in cash. Bakers bringing bread to the village had to pay their toll in loaves. Centuries earlier, Macduff, fleeing to his castle near Lindores after the murder of Macbeth, had to cross the Tay at Inchyra. Having no money in his possession, he is said to have paid his ferry fare with a loaf of bread. The custom of accepting bread as currency in the village gave rise to the naming of the passage as 'The Loaf Ferry'. It continued to function until well into the nineteenth century. In the early days of steam, two paddle boats, the *Star of Gowrie* and the *Lass of Gowrie*, were employed on the passage, but in 1847, when the railways began to take away trade, the demand for the ferry diminished. One boat, the *Emily Florence*, sailed on for a number of years in the twentieth century, often transporting grain and potatoes, but eventually this boat too had to be discontinued.

The last ferry passage to be found on the Tay east of Perth was that between Easter Rhynd, sited at the eastern foot of the Moncreiffe Hill, and Kinfauns on the north bank. Two boats served this passage; the larger transported horses 'and other bestial', while the smaller boat carried foot passengers. As time passed, this ferry was less frequented, the piers fell into disrepair and, by the mid-nineteenth century, there was little or no demand for a service. Nevertheless, in the second half of the nineteenth century, with the introduction of large steamers, a small rowing boat was kept to convey passengers to and from these boats plying daily between Dundee and Perth and unable to dock at the unsafe, inadequate pier at Kinfauns. Records do not relate whether or not these steam boats observed the old custom connected with Kinfauns Castle. In 1688, a large iron vane, with the date cut in the middle, was erected on the top of the castle as the mark of a heritable office or power of Admiralty over the river annexed to the estate of Kinfauns for preserving the fishing on the Tay with the authority to punish any who poached or destroyed the salmon. In accordance with tradition, all vessels passing up and down the Tay were required to acknowledge the status of the owners of the estate by giving a salute or by lowering their colours to the castle.

It was not until the late twentieth century that two major bridges, rail and road, were constructed over the Tay estuary. The building of these bridges, at great expense and incorporating the most modern technology, acknowledged the importance of maintaining communication links in this area once served by so many ferries. The role of the Tay estuary ferries, greater and lesser, may only be fully appreciated in retrospect.

CHAPTER 5

Northern Firths Ferries

The Firths of Moray, Cromarty and Dornoch are broad parallel stretches of the North Sea which penetrate the land mass of the north-east corner of Scotland. From early times, some ferry crossings over these firths were necessary to the religious, military, and commercial life of these parts. As early as 563 A.D., Christianity reached this area of Scotland when Columba braved the hardships of travel to pay a visit to the Pictish King Brude at the vitrified fort on the hill of Craig Phadraig, near Inverness. Thereafter, the influence of Christianity grew and was reinforced in the thirteenth and fourteenth centuries with the erection of the cathedrals at Dornoch and Fortrose as well as the abbey at Fearn. Moreover, Vikings and Norsemen from the islands of Orkney and Shetland took advantage of the access provided by these firths to raid the surrounding lands. When Malcolm Canmore, in the eleventh century, married Ingibjorg, daughter of the great Earl Thorfinn, a more peaceful period ensued. In the sixteenth and seventeenth centuries, when trading increased, regular ferry services across the firths became vital, but in spite of this, little or no money was spent on improving the facilties and the ferries remained rough and ready and often dangerous. Even after the 1745 Jacobite uprising little change occurred, although Fort George was built at Ardersier on the south shore of the Moray Firth to house troops employed in maintaining law and order in the Highlands. This replaced General Wade's earlier fortification at Inverness which had been destroyed by Prince Charles Edward's forces.

The village of Ardersier came to prominence only after 1748 with the completion of Fort George, although, according to the Rev. Charles Cordiner, it rapidly became 'a mere useless memorial to the state of that turbulent period'. Today, the Fort is still used as a barracks but mainly houses the regimental museum of the Queen's Own Highlanders. The headland on which the Fort is built, together with the promontory, Chanory Point, on the opposite side of the Firth, narrows the channel of water, thus providing an appropriate place for a ferry crossing. In the thirteenth and early fourteenth centuries, the ferry was particularly busy as it constantly transported workmen employed in building Fortrose Cathedral. In 1657, the Register of the Great Seal records that 'Heugh Fraser, eldest lawful son to Thomas Fraser of Eskidaill is granted the ale-house and ferry boatts at Channorie'. Almost a hundred years later, in 1746, the ferry boat at Ardersier was part of a marriage contract between Elizabeth Grant, daughter of Sir James Grant of Grant, then proprietor of the ferry, and Hugh Rose of Kilravock, thus keeping the ferry under the jurisdiction of the family.

There appear to have been few accidents on this passage, which is remarkable on such an exposed stretch of water when the boat was small and relied on an inadequate sail and two oars for propulsion. A tragedy did occur one stormy November day in 1811 when thirteen people and a pony were on board. In rough seas the boat capsized and only two of the passengers were saved. The lost boat was replaced and continued to provide transport for the public, workmen and soldiers stationed at Fort George. In the 1930s, Alexander McLean, the ferryman at that time, was held in such high regard that an article written about him was published in the September issue of *Caber Feidh*, the regimental magazine of the Seaforth Highlanders. 'Alec', as he was called, was said to have become 'part of the Moray Firth'. Born in Kessock, he worked on the Kessock ferry as a lad, spent eighteen years on the Balblair to Invergordon ferry and finally came to Chanonry Point in 1912, where he worked first under John Hossack, the senior ferryman, and later undertook the total responsibility for the ferry. The article related that Alec was 'a simple and happy man' whose philosophy included such precepts as 'There is no music except that which God gave us; there is no art except nature and a man's heaven is here on earth'. Alec was a bachelor who lived with his sister in a small cottage near the Chanonry lighthouse and, like most ferrymen, he was not averse to enjoying a few drams. Sadly, this inclination proved to be his downfall. His friend, Alec Cameron, a retired joiner living in Ardersier, was able to recall the occasion.

Mr. Cameron used the ferry frequently, as he worked at Fortrose. One stormy winter's day, with a gale blowing and snow driving, he arrived at Chanonry Point to board the ferry as usual, but Alec was reluctant to set off in such conditions. However, the storm abated and the pair decided to risk the crossing in the lull that ensued. After some hard rowing they arrived safely at the other side, although Alec was forced to beach the boat between the Quarters and the Fort instead of at the normal landing quay at Fort George. That night Alec met up with a crony, a sergeant stationed at the Fort, and together they visited the Sergeants' Mess. Alec imbibed too heartily and when he left the Mess he was seen to be drunk. The following day, Alec's body was found on the beach at Fortrose. It was assumed that although he must have made a successful crossing, he then fell into the water when attempting to land at Chanonry Point. As a result of Alec's death and because there was no ferryman sufficiently skilled to undertake the job, the ferry service ceased for a time. Then three local men, Charlie More, John Smith and John Sutherland, combined to employ a small motor launch on the passage but lack of demand soon undermined this venture and the ferry operated no longer.

In the Moray Firth, the major ferry passage was at Kessock from the tip of the Merkynche, opposite Inverness Castle, to North Kessock. Originally, this passage lay at the point where the Moray and the Beauly Firths meet and it made an important link between Inverness and the most northerly counties of Scotland. On 4th September 1437, the ferry right of Kessock was granted to the prior and friars of the Dominican monastery of Inverness by Alexander de Isle, Earl of Ross and Lord of the Isles, for 'the salvation of his soul'. At the same time, the lands and ferry on the north side of the firth were part of the estate of Redcastle, with an annual rent of twenty shillings Scots being payable to the burgh of Inverness for the privilege. The strategic position of the Kessock ferry, near to Inverness Castle, made it a significant factor in any conflict occurring in the area. In 1649, when Cromwell was making a bid to control Scotland, Royalist troops, mostly drawn from the Mackenzie and Mackay clans, surprised and overcame the Inverness garrison left by Fraser of Beauly to defend Bishop's Castle at Fortrose. The successful Highlanders advanced towards Inverness and overcame those left to guard the Kessock ferry. Using the ferry boats to transport the troops, and cunningly utilising the element of surprise, the Highlanders caught the defence forces unawares and compelled the surrender of the castle.

The ferry was a cheap mode of transport for troops as soldiers were traditionally carried free of charge. Other concessions were often included in different localities, and if these were ignored by the ferrymen, complaints were not long in being voiced. In 1719, for example, Lord Strathnaver accused the Laird of Redcastle, the proprietor of the Kessock ferry, of charging his workmen the full ferry fare. Lord Strathnaver wrote, 'soldiers and such workmen had the privilege to go free at all ferries within the kingdom'. Lord Strathnaver sent peremptory orders, therefore, that 'not only must free passage be given to the pioneers but also the money unlawfully taken must be returned'. Later that year, Lord Strathnaver again referred to the Kessock ferry in equally dictatorial tones. He directed the deputy-lieutenant of Moray and Ross to raise a regiment by sending 'six score men, with proper officers, to meet at the Kessock ferry not later than the following Saturday'. These men were to be followed by another six score on successive Saturdays until sufficient numbers had been raised. These troops were to be used to protect the new defences being built at Inverness to contain any future uprising. In the event of the 1745 uprising, little use was made of these fortifications. The Kessock ferry, in common with a number of other ferries plying on the estuaries of the north-east at that time, was used to facilitate the movement of troops and played a part in the strategic plans of both sides. On 18th February 1746, Lord Loudoun decided to use the Kessock ferry to pursue the rebel forces into Ross and Cromarty. He planned a ruse designed to outwit the rebels. He left Inverness with a few companies and marched them ostentatiously eastwards. The main body of his troops were retained at the ferry and boarded the boats but the rebels got wind of this manoeuvre and were well positioned on the north shore of the Firth to await their arrival. Lord Loudoun's men were sitting targets for the rebels and it is little wonder that, of those who survived, at least 250 men deserted.

In 1746, throughout the countryside surrounding Inverness, the feeling of uncertainty increased with the withdrawal northwards of Prince Charles and his diminishing forces. Government troops were gathered to confront the Jacobites and the Lord President, Duncan Forbes of Culloden, together with Lord Loudoun and others, was resident at Culloden House. A group of rebels planned to take Culloden House by storm and capture the inmates. A Highlander, Coll Bain, was privy to this information but he owed a favour to the Lord President who had been instrumental in acquitting him of a murder charge. Therefore Bain forced a woman minding sheep near Culloden House to take a letter of warning to Duncan Forbes. On receiving the message, the President reacted quickly and the whole of his entourage succeeded in escaping by way of Kessock ferry. They hid in the hills of Ross-shire until after the battle of Culloden when they were able to emerge and return in safety.

In the late eighteenth century, with the increase in the movement of people and goods, ferry services came under greater scrutiny than before. Sir John Sinclair, the great agriculturist with lands in Ross and Cromarty, was free with his comments regarding ferries. He concluded that if 'a stranger from a more enlightened country perused our boats, their internal arrangement, tackle and apparel and the dexterous skill of our navigations, he certainly could not but admire our confident boldness in the first instance; but he must sadly deplore our scandalous neglect and unambitious supineness'.

At the beginning of the nineteenth century, changes did take place on both sides of the Kessock ferry. Grant, Laird of Redcastle and proprietor of the ferry, proposed a scheme to improve the north landing site. A pier and an inn were to be built, together with a new access road. On the south side, the ferry location was moved about a mile to the east of Inverness and a new quay was to be erected there. These plans were implemented and an improved service resulted. At that time, there was no provision for the increasing traffic in wheeled vehicles. Horses still had to be unhitched and taken separately from carriages and carts, causing delays and inconvenience. More money was required to buy bigger and more easily managed boats. To raise money Sir John Sinclair suggested that, in spite of the improvements already carried out by the Laird of Redcastle, the public would be better served if the ferry was owned by a company. Sir John proposed that twenty-six gentlemen of the county should each subscribe £500. He argued that such an investment would lead to greater use of the ferry, resulting in more income from fares, thus providing funds for improvements and, in turn, offering a better service to the public. This logic fell on deaf ears and the lairds of Redcastle continued to own the ferry and to do their utmost to provide the best possible service. Occasionally, the ferrymen were the recipients of largesse distributed by several gentlemen of the county. In the early nineteenth century, Duncan Davidson of Tulloch, a tall handsome young man said to be generous to a fault, frequently paid the ferryman a sovereign for his fare instead of the statutory penny. This was no hardship to young Davidson who succeeded to Tulloch Castle and estates near Dingwall, as well as inheriting £60,000 cash, together with £7,000 per annum from land rents. Of course, welcome hand-outs to the ferryman did nothing to improve the facilities at the ferry as these continued to be the responsibility of the proprietor. In 1811, Southey found the Kessock ferry 'the best in Scotland' but added, 'But the best ferry is a bad thing. They have no means of getting carriages on board and there is condiderable difficulty with one of the horses'. In 1825, Sir William Fettes purchased the Redcastle estate including the rights of ferry at Kessock. To keep abreast of developments at other ferries in Scotland, it was proposed to employ a steam boat but difficulties arose concerning suitable landing places, so yawls and pinnaces continued to be used.

The ferrymen took pride in the good safety record and reputation enjoyed by the ferry at Kessock but in 1846, on a boisterous morning in July, a ferryman was drowned. William Mackay, the ferryman, was sitting on the edge of the boat holding a horse's head, but when halfway across the horse suddenly took fright, reared up and leapt overboard, at the same time toppling Mackay into the water. Both man and beast might have been saved had not the horse been wearing a martingale which severely restricted any free movement of its head, thus preventing it from swimming ashore and carrying the ferryman to safety. Again, on a rough day in February in 1854, Alexander Mackenzie, tacksman of the ferry, was drowned as he assisted in the mooring of one of the ferry boats.

The more recent history of the Kessock ferry shows that the service was beset by constant money problems. In the late nineteenth and early twentieth centuries, change in the ownership of the ferry emphasised the financial vulnerability of operating such a service. In 1899, Sir Donald Macdonald purchased the ferry and leased it to John Finlayson of Nairn at a rent of £500 per annum. The Kessock Ferry Company Ltd. undertook the lease in 1906, and in 1907 a steam ferry

Two nineteenth century ferryboats wait at the quay at Invergordon to cross the Cromarty Firth to Balblair. At that time, the main post road to Kessock and Inverness passed through Invergordon village where the excellent inn was no doubt an attraction to the many travellers who arrived both by coach and by boat.

boat was put on the passage for the very first time. In 1921, The New Kessock Ferry Company took the lease. This company comprised Provost Macdonald of Inverness and his two sons who successfully ran the service using a twin-screw passenger boat with facilities for transporting cars. In 1935, an application was made, and consent given, for the employment of a chain boat. Unfortunately, this permission was never implemented as three chain boats sank while en route to Kessock. Indeed, the only ferry boat in operation between 1935 and 1939 was a small motor boat, much to the disgust of the travelling public who were deprived of any adequate means of transport across the Firth. Finally, in 1939, the right of ferry was acquired by the County Council of Ross and Cromarty, together with Inverness Town Council. Immediately, *The Hope* was purchased at a cost of £1,180. This was a steam-powered vessel capable of carrying vehicles and passengers but it was already twenty-two years

old. Wartime conditions, increased running costs, difficulties
in recruiting a suitable crew and the poor condition of *The
Hope* combined to incur a not inconsiderable debt. In 1948,
the review of ferries report recommended an increase in the
five-car capacity boat and went as far as concluding that 'a
bridge will be required ultimately'.

In 1961, between June and September the ferry boat, with
a capacity for eight to ten cars, carried 38,642 cars and
120,021 passengers with a charge of 3/6d for each car. Clearly,
the demand for transport across the Firth was on the increase,
and by 1972 the need to build a bridge had been accepted by
the authorities and plans were made. Even in 1978, when the
bridge was being constructed, there were problems at the
ferry. In February that year, an emergency bus service had
to be arranged to run between the Black Isle and Inverness
to compensate for the withdrawal of the ferry boat *Eilean
Dubh* which had been damaged. The two-hourly bus service
was hardly comparable to the customary half-hourly ferry
service and the public protested vigorously until the ferry
service was restored. It was no doubt with a sense of relief as
well as a feeling of pride that the local community greeted
the opening of the Kessock Bridge in 1982, while at the same
time bidding a nostalgic farewell to the ferry boats that had
served them for so long.

The Cromarty Firth, dividing the Black Isle from the
county of Ross, is described by Hugh Millar, Cromarty's
most famous son, as 'a gigantic wall of brown precipices,
beetling for many miles over the edge of the firth'. These
shores were not conducive to easy landings from ferry boats,
but crossings were essential as the only alternative was a
tedious circumnavigation by way of Dingwall. The bay of
Cromarty is a fine natural harbour which has provided a safe
shelter for shipping down the ages. In 1785, a large new quay
was built to accommodate vessels of over 350 tons, and
simultaneously it afforded an unusually good landing place
for ferry boats. Cromarty was the ferry terminal for boats
plying to Dunskeath/Nigg and to Invergordon. In the early

nineteenth century, further extensions were made when a new pier 90 yards long was erected at Cromarty.

In the fifteenth century, the Cromarty to Dunskeath ferry was known as 'The King's Ferry' because revenue from it assisted in the upkeep of the royal castle at Dunskeath. At that time, Scottish kings took note of this 'King's Ferry'. James II directed moneys gathered from the ferry towards the maintenance of the chaplaincy at Tain, while James IV travelled across the passage in 1497 and 1501. Over the years, the two ferry boats gave a useful service to the community with one being used to convey beasts and vehicles while the other, a smaller boat, took only passengers. By 1906, according to the *Thorough Guide to the Northern Highlands*, a steam launch, 'presented by Mr. Carnegie' (presumably Andrew Carnegie, the great philanthropist), took six minutes to carry passengers, cycles and motor cycles across the narrows at a cost of 2d, 4d and 1/— respectively. In 1914, the fares had risen to 6d, 1/6d and 2/—. The 1948 review considered there was no need to employ a larger vessel to carry cars. Albert Watson, MBE, retired from the post of ferryman at Cromarty in the 1970s. He was a small, square-shouldered man with the natural sailor's keen eye and weather-worn face. After over forty years sailing around the Cromarty Firth, his memories centred on spectacular gatherings of the British fleet in halcyon pre-1939 days. He recalled the servicemen he had ferried and the wartime years when he was paid £36 per month by the Post Office for deliveries which involved travelling 10,000 miles in a year. The MBE, presented to him by the late Duchess of Kent, was awarded because he had risked his life several times. On the first occasion, he harnessed and then towed away two live mines, over a ton of explosive, which had drifted into Cromarty harbour. On the second occasion, he was ferrying members of a boys' football team unaware that the boat had been damaged below the water line; when the boat began to sink, he managed to save the lives of six boys although three did drown. Finally, he was a member of the crew of the Cromarty lifeboat for thirty-four years, many of them as coxswain, and took part in innumerable rescues. When Albert retired in the mid-1970s, the oil industry, then expanding, was the source of prosperity in the area and ferry traffic increased. Today, only a passenger boat plies this passage. A ferry also exists between Cromarty and Invergordon, although little documentation can be found regarding its history. In 1909, D. T. Holmes refers to a 'wee, puffing, hard-wrought steam-launch' plying the passage, but no recommendation for any change was made in the ferry review in 1948 and today travellers can still catch this ferry boat.

The narrowness of the crossing from Balblair to Inver-gordon makes this three-quarters of a mile stretch of water a natural ferry point. As early as 1618, there was reference to the 'Ferryton near Balblair' in the Urquhart papers, although there was no landing place at that time. Only in 1821 was a new quay built and it was exceptionally long at 130 yards. Two more wooden piers were constructed in 1857 as, by then, Balblair was flourishing as a stopping point for the steamboat traffic arriving from Inverness, Aberdeen and Leith. Invergordon, a lively town with an excellent inn, also benefited from the boom in steamboat travel, especially as there was a link with coaches using the new post road through the Black Isle to Inverness. There were at least two ferry boats in use at Invergordon, one for carrying horses and carriages, while the other transported foot passengers. When cars were first on the roads in the early 1900s, two planks were placed on the boat to ferry them across the water, one at a time, at a cost of 2/6d each. A precarious exercise! By 1914, putting safety before convenience, cars were no longer allowed to be transported, and since then only a passenger service has been running. In 1979, the completion of the Cromarty Bridge, which spans the Firth, greatly reduced the need for ferries, and the few still in use cater mainly for workers in the oil business.

The three known remaining ferries on the Cromarty Firth are those at Alness, Foulis and Alcaig. These are ancient

The ferry passage over Loch Fleet at Little Ferry formed a direct link in the chain of ferry crossings between Inverness and Golspie where the earls of Sutherland held sway in Dunrobin Castle.

ferries that have consistently provided a local service without attracting much attention. According to the Statistical Account, the ferry at Foulis was 'not a much frequented ferry and is incommodious at low water from the shallowness of the shore'. The Alcaig ferry, which boasted a large and a small boat, was also at the mercy of the tide, and although the passage could sometimes be forded, at other times it was 'a hazard', especially as it was said that hardly a year passed without a life being lost.

According to information received from R. W. Fraser, the Dingwall to Alcaig ferry was still being used at the beginning of the twentieth century when Charlie Mackenzie and his sister Jess were in charge. They were known as 'Charlie and Jess the Ferry'. Charlie's sons, William and Jock, nicknamed Jumbo, succeeded their father and aunt, ferrying until well into the 1930s and always charging 2d per passenger. The Mackenzies lived in a cottage on the Dingwall side of the ferry beside a wooden jetty which gave access to the boat. An open-fronted lean-to gave waiting passengers shelter, a thoughtful provision on occasions when the ferry was delayed due to personal business pursued by the ferrymen when on the opposite side. The boat was a coble, flat-bottomed and propelled by the ferryman using two oars. The grave of 'Jock (Jumbo) the Ferry' can be found in the old churchyard at Dingwall.

The obvious point to cross the exposed and treacherous Dornoch Firth was the narrow passage at the Meikle ferry. The Great North Road, connecting with the Meikle ferry, was shortest route to Thurso and Wick but the dangers experienced at the ferry often persuaded travellers to take the much longer but safer way via the Bonar Bridge. Not only was the Meikle ferry a notorious crossing but the vagaries of the tide frequently left boats stranded on sandbanks. One of the first references to the Meikle ferry, known earlier as Portincoulter, is in a charter dated 4th March 1560, by Alan Ross of Balnagowan in favour of Donald Dingwall, natural son of Alexander Dingwall, prebendary chaplain of Cambuscurry, who was no doubt aware of the strategic value of the ferry location.

During the seventeenth century, when both the pros and cons of the Covenanting cause were receiving local support, the Meikle ferry was frequently used for the transportation of troops. The captive Marquis of Montrose was hustled across the ferry on his way to Tain, the south and subsequent death. A century later during the 1745 uprising, the ferry man, McGill, acted as a reliable spy for the government by reporting the positions held by the rebel forces. Eventually, he suffered retribution when his ferry boats were destroyed and only escaped with his life. Nevertheless, his information enabled Lords Loudoun and Forbes to organise the assembly of all available ferry boats at the Tain side of the ferry in order to evacuate their troops at the most appropriate time, thus taking the Jacobite forces by surprise.

Towards the end of the eighteenth century, the Statistical Account states that the Meikle ferry was served, on each side, by 'a large boat for transporting carriages, horses and other cattle; as also a yawl for the accommodation of foot passengers'. Cattle were encouraged to swim over the passage but often the beasts refused to go into the water because it was so cold. Consequently, they had to be ferried across, causing much delay and extra effort. It is said that drovers could foretell the outcome of the market according to the willingness of the cattle to swim or not; if the beasts swam, prices would be high, but if not, there would be little profit. By the beginning of the next century, the Meikle ferry had been worked by three generations of the Patience family but they had seen few improvements during that time. The boats were in a poor state with frayed ropes, torn sails and defective rudders; there was no proper quay for landing and delays were insufferable even to the most tolerant traveller. Strong arguments for the building of a bridge were consistently ignored until, in 1812, Telford erected an iron bridge at Bonar at a cost of £13,971. This was built after a public outcry at conditions at the Meikle ferry following an appalling accident there in 1809. James Mitchell, the famous civil engineer, unwittingly witnessed the scene as he arrived too late to catch the ferry boat which had just set sail.

Late in the afternoon of 16th August 1809, the day of the great Lammas Fair in Tain, Hugh McCulloch, sheriff-substitute, came to the Meikle ferry. The shore was crowded with people returning home from the fair. On McCulloch's arrival he was quickly seated in the stern of the ferry yawl followed by a pushing, pressing throng all anxious to be taken across the water. McCulloch became apprehensive about the numbers crowding aboard and even turned away about forty folk. Still the boat was overladen but the water was dead calm and the ferrymen set sail. When the boat was halfway across the passage water gushed in, the boat sank and ninety-nine people drowned, including the sheriff-substitute; only twelve survived. Another accident occurred on 28th October 1835 when the ferry boat was holed and sank. On this occasion there were seventeen passengers aboard but only one, J. H. Richardson, a shipping secretary from North Shields, was drowned. The ferryman showed great presence of mind by using a small boat moored nearby to rescue the remainder of the passengers.

In spite of these tragedies and the building of the bridge at Bonar, traffic at the Meikle ferry continued to be sufficiently heavy to merit a design by Stevenson for a bridge over the Dornoch Firth. However, as no money was forthcoming to build the bridge, the project was abandoned. Even the mail coach, drawn by two horses, used the ferry until the 1850s when the increasing delays dictated re-routing via Bonar Bridge. Still the ferry continued to operate, and in the early twentieth century the Contour Guide books gave clear directions to travellers: 'The boats are on the north side. Hoist flag on the south side. This is an exposed ferry and useless in stormy weather'. There was a further warning: 'Motor cars carried when water suits the big boat only'. Subsequently, only passengers were carried, with the 1948 review concluding that 'there is not sufficient demand . . . for the institution of a vehicular ferry . . .'. It was not until 8th January 1986 that the long-awaited promise of a bridge was pledged with the announcement of a competition for the design of a bridge over the Dornoch Firth. It is to be 800 metres long and will cost between £11 million and £16 million approximately. Although the completion of this bridge will no doubt be welcomed by local people and travellers alike, the ancient Meikle ferry will always have an important place in the history of Easter Ross.

Two additional ferries were employed on passages over the narrow entrance to Loch Fleet at Little Ferry and at the 'port of Unes' on Lake Unes north of Dornoch. One boat at Little Ferry was served by four ferrymen but the ferry came briefly to prominence during the 1745 uprising only. In 1746, the Earl of Cromarty and his men were urgently summoned to join Prince Charles Edward at Inverness, but when they reached Little Ferry they were suddenly attacked. In the confusion the Earl and his officers retreated hastily to

Dunrobin Castle but the men crammed into the only available ferry boat to try to escape. The boat became quickly overcrowded, and those who could not climb aboard clung on to the sides to be pulled through the water. The boat was in great danger of capsizing until those soldiers who were aboard drew their dirks and hacked off the fingers of the others clinging to the gunwales. Many died. The following day, the Battle of Culloden was fought and perhaps the lack of reinforcements from the north due to this adversity may have contributed to the defeat of the Prince.

The ferry boat at Lake Unes was in use by 1467 when Margaret, Countess of Sutherland, a daughter of the Earl of Ross, Lord of the Isles, was returning home to Dunrobin Castle at Golspie. Her husband John, the third Earl of Sutherland, recorded that when the Countess was on the ferry in the middle of the passage, a severe storm arose, overturning the boat and throwing the lady into the water. She was washed up on the shore, still 'with some lyff in her'. There she was found by a fugitive, John Dairg, who recognised her as someone of great importance. For some unknown reason he 'promptly dispatched her', then fled, but had little chance of escape as the distraught Earl carried out a thorough search for his wife's murderer. John Dairg was executed almost as soon as the Countess was buried in the churchyard at Golspie. The ferry continued to operate, with records showing that, in 1630, the annual rent for the privilege of leasing the passage boat was 40 bolls of barley 'to be delivered at the ferry of Unes or the girnel of Golspie'.

The replacement of ferries by bridges on these north-eastern estuaries has spanned many decades, from the building of the Bonar Bridge over the Dornoch Firth in 1812 to the anticipated completion of the Dornoch Bridge in the late 1980s. Current, sophisticated, convenient travel across all these firths cannot blot out the memory of the struggle, effort and sacrifice that bedevilled the ferry services which provided access to the most northerly parts of Scotland.

CHAPTER 6

Sea Loch Ferries

Sea lochs on the west coast of Scotland were formed by glacial activity which, in this area, resulted in the sea penetrating the land mass. These long and mostly narrow indentations are open to the fury of the tides and storms of the Atlantic at one end and are often confined between rising hills at the other. Ferries were frequently located at the shortest crossing points where the land was low-lying. The combined effect of the strong tides and the narrowness of the channels made these crossings dangerous and difficult. Until the nineteenth century, roads in the West Highland region were few, ill-defined and little frequented, and the importance of sea-loch ferries was given little recognition outside their own locality. It was only following the expansion of the cattle trade, the export of kelp and easier passage made possible by the introduction of steam-powered boats that such ferries attracted any attention. Even then, little was done to improve the amenities until the demands of the growing vehicular traffic in the mid-twentieth century forced changes to be made.

Loch Fyne sweeps between promontories of land from the Sound of Bute to the inlet of the river Fyne near Cairndow. The principal ferries were located at East Otter, Creggans and Inveraray and these supported the commercial enterprises arising from the natural resources of timber and herring which had long been plentiful on the shores and in the waters of the loch. Furthermore, the castle at Inveraray was the seat of the Earls of Argyll, chiefs of the Clan Campbell, a formidable factor in Scottish history.

In the eighteenth century, the ferry passage at East Otter, at the south end of Loch Fyne, terminated on the Silvercraigs

One of the regular Clyde steamers from Glasgow moored at Inveraray pier in the 1930s. The popularity of such excursions not only promoted tourism but opened up the national beauties of western Scotland to those hitherto bound by the drudgery of work in the cities.

estate at Port Ann on the west bank. Silvercraigs was owned by the Lamont family and, in 1747, Angus Lamont, a younger son, joined forces with James Black, the son of the Otter ferryman, known as 'the most audacious smuggler in all the country'. They were caught but the verdict was 'Not Proven'. Somewhat unfairly, James Black's father was penalised by being removed as the ferryman at Otter to be replaced by Daniel Luke. Angus Lamont's father, William, a pillar of respectability as a member of the Commissioners of Supply

Committee, nevertheless signed an order 'to disable and break all boats . . . not belonging to common ferries', such as those at Creggans and other nearby locations, thereby attempting a monopoly of ferry trade for himself. His instructions were ignored and the ferries concerned continued to operate as before. In 1782, William's son, Archibald Lamont, built a ferry house of the following dimensions: '16' broad within walls; 27' to 30' long within walls, well thatched with heather'. It doubled as an inn and cost five guineas.

From the mid-eighteenth century, the local Commissioners of Supply Committee took heed of the state of the ferries on Loch Fyne although their recommendations were not always implemented. Concerning the Otter ferry, orders were given to improve quays at both sides of the passage but the money allocated to the Lamonts of Silvercraig was not used for that purpose. Always in need of cash, the Lamonts spent money from any source whatever. Thus, the ferry quays at Otter continued to deteriorate and complaints were made, particularly at the height of the black cattle trade. Nevertheless, the Lamonts still strongly claimed their right to match the ferry rates at Otter with those at Creggans and Inveraray. In 1770, fares were fixed at 6d for a single man and 9d for a man and his horse and these rates remained for many years. The Otter ferry boat was never upgraded to transport wheeled traffic, and by the late nineteenth century the boat sailed only from the east side; a fire had to be lit at Port Ann to summon ferrymen to the west shore for passengers waiting there. The charges had risen to 1/— per passenger and 6d for a bicycle, now more common than a horse. The 1948 review of ferries examined the possibility of providing a ferry boat capable of transporting vehicles but concluded that no change was justified. Furthermore, the improvement of the steamer service from the Clyde to Loch Fyne was a factor in the eventual demise of the ferry at Otter.

In 1650, the combined parishes of Strathlachlan and Strachur on Loch Fyne were served by a ferry located at Creggans, about half-a-mile from Strachur where an ancient

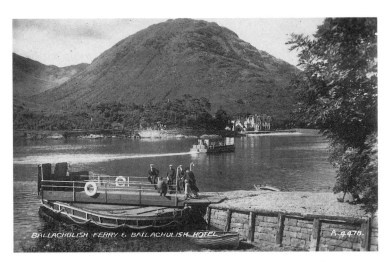

In the late 1940s a two-car ferryboat was operating on the passage over Loch Linnhe. The well-constructed quay, the larger boat and the more sophisticated turntable device indicated the improvements necessary to meet the heavy demands imposed on the Ballachulish ferry service to accommodate the ever-increasing volume of traffic.

custom, dating from the Crusades, still continued. The lairds of the two parishes were soldiers-in-arms in the Holy Land and they made a pact that the survivor would carry the head of his companion home to be buried in the churchyard at Strachur. This came to pass and thereafter, through the centuries, one laird would always 'lay his neighbour's head in the grave'.

In 1563, Mary, Queen of Scots, a guest of the Earl of Argyll at Inverarary Castle, was attracted by Strachur. During a royal hunt near the village the Queen shot a stag before returning to Inverarary by the Creggans ferry boat. Such dignitaries travelled free although others of lesser degree who regularly used the ferry paid partly by a 'victual stent (3 bolls of corn) payable from neighbouring farms' and partly by 'a Trifle of money payable by Strangers passing this way', viz: '2d Stg for a single passenger, 4d Stg for a man and a horse, 2d Stg for a Cow when bound and laid and 2½d Stg when standing'. The ferry at Creggans continued until the nineteenth century when a new road was constructed between Creggans and St. Catherine's providing readier access to Inverarary.

The ferry from Inverarary to St. Catherine's was the best-administered and also the best documented ferry in the area. This is not surprising as it operated close to Inverarary Castle and was constantly used by the Earls of Argyll and their households. From 1680, records refer to conditions established for ferry tacks or leases. It was 'ordained that John Murray, ferrier, must either find caution to keep up the new ferry boat delivered to him and to redeliver the same back in good condition or to demit his charge as ferrier and that betwixt now and Tuesday next to come'. In 1710, the Earl of Argyll allocated the ferry tack by 'public roup' to Donald Clark at an annual rent of £20 Scots. This tack included 'the haile emoluments and perquisites of house and yard' but was subject to a penalty of £40 if the conditions were not met. In 1725, the annual rent was increased to £50 Scots per annum or the 'highest offer', and the boat was to be 'two strokes higher than the old one'. Alex McDugald, the ferryman, was to 'purchase for the same a mast, Sail and oars, cables, anchor and Ridder as sufficient with other Furniture'. In addition to ferrying duties, he was engaged to 'attend to the Gounknock [clock] and keep the same going regularly ... and also to toll the Town Clock regularly ... every morning at six and every night at Ten of the Clock'. Furthermore, 'the magistrates, minister and town clerk and other members of the Town Council will be ferried gratis except what they please to give of good will'. Different sizes of boat were available at the ferry; a yawl transported horses and cattle and later carriages, while rowing boats conveyed passengers and goods.

By the late nineteenth century, Joseph Mitchell, the civil engineer, referred to a new ferry boat, 'a small steamer' which 'has brought us across the ferry three miles and landed

MOTOR BOAT CROSSING BALLACHULISH FERRY

In the early 1920s a motor ferryboat was employed at the Ballachulish ferry. This boat had an elementary turntable to load and unload the single vehicle it was capable of carrying.

us safely on the quay at Inverarary' in full view of the beautiful grounds of Inveraray Castle earlier dubbed 'Argyll's bowling green' by Alexander Carlyle.

In the eighteenth century, the fifth Duke of Argyll built a new town at Inveraray and introduced new industries to stimulate different and more profitable work. The venture was unsuccessful and it was not until the late nineteenth century, when regular steamer services from the Clyde were established, that tourism flourished and brought work and some prosperity in its wake. The twentieth century brought its own problems for the ferry which was unable to keep up with the demands created by the growth in vehicular traffic. Between 1946 and 1962, a motor ferry launch plied across the passage three times a day and linked up with coach services to Dunoon. The recruitment of ferrymen became difficult, and when no suitable person was available the ferry was discontinued.

Problems facing ferrymen on Loch Fyne were different
from those experienced on Loch Etive which divides the
districts of Lorne and Benderloch by narrow straits at Connel
and Bonawe where ferries were located. The narrowness of
the passage at Connel, together with a sunken reef of rocks,
causes turbulence in the water, especially at an ebb tide. This
whirlpool, known as the Falls of Lora, created problems of
navigation for ferrymen. In 1799, Sarah Murray noted in her
journal, *The Beauties of Scotland*, that these eddies 'will
sometimes turn a ferry boat quite round, half round and zig-
zag three or four times in its passage across and yet it will be
in perfect safety'. This description was echoed by John
Stoddard in his *Local Survey and Manners in Scotland in 1799
and 1800* when he commented, 'It is a safer ferry than many of
more placid look; no accident has been known in living
memory and it is very entertaining to behold the dexterous
navigation of the small boats skirting the edge of the
whirlpools, apparently the sport of their violence but in fact,
assisted by their strength'. Traditionally, the Falls of Lora
are associated with Deirdre, the beautiful legendary Irish
heroine, whose dun, or iron-age homestead, was said to have
been built in Glen Etive at Dalness, 'the field of the waterfall',
where she lived with her lover, Naoise.

The ferry at Connel was one of those 'putt under securitie
and good cautione' in 1681 by order of the Privy Council in
an attempt to check the traffic in stolen cattle. Captain Burt
indicated in his *Letters* the difficulties encountered in
transporting beasts at any time: 'There is a boat . . . not large
enough to receive a Horse; and therefore he is swum at the
Stern, while somebody holds up his Head by Halter or
Bridle . . . if the Water be wide and they [the horses] generally
turn themselves on one of their sides and patiently suffer
themselves to be dragged along'. In the nineteenth century,
John McCulloch told Sir Walter Scott that those 'who drive
gigs and barouches have only to lament that the ferry at
Connel is not so convenient to exit and entrance as a few
pounds put on landing places might have made them'. He

The Ferry   1906

At the Ballachulish ferry on Loch Linnhe in 1906 cars were driven from the quay along two narrow wooden planks which straddled the gunwhales of the ferryboat. It was a considerable feat on the part of the driver in conjunction with the ferrymen to achieve the precarious balance necessary.

added ruefully, 'He who comes to Connel ferry will require a large share of patientia ferryboatica', as 'a Highland horse does not choose to take his seat in a boat . . . neither recte nor rectro, nor blindfolded . . .'. He continued, 'The Athenians committed a blunder when they made Neptune the progenitor of horses . . . I would feed my horse on pitch and tar till he had learnt to land, reef and steer'.

Dorothy Wordsworth recounted the problems she met at Connel in 1803: 'the horse was unyolked and being harshly driven over rough stones, which were as slippery as ice with shiny seaweed, he was in terror before he reached the boat and then [the man] completed the work by beating him and pushing him by main force over the ridge of the boat . . . a blackguard looking fellow, blind in one eye, held him by force like a horse-breaker while the poor creature fretted and stamped . . . the motion of the boat and the noise and foam of the waves terrified him . . . when we were all far enough from the shore to be drowned, he became furious and plunged desperately, his hind legs in the water, then, recovering himself, he beat with such force against the side of the boat we were afraid he should send his foot through. The men were swearing terrible oaths . . . and when we reached the landing-place they whipped him ashore in brutal triumph'.

In the 1820s, a new quay was built at Connel costing £118/15/−. In 1833, the Road Trustees Committee decreed that the ferry boats must be kept available on the south side of the passage to obviate delay and inconvenience although the ferry inn was sited on the north side where it is still a hotel. At first, the construction of a railway bridge in the 1890s afforded little competition for the ferry. The first cars were transported by train, 'without petrol and storage batteries', at a fare of 7/6d, while passengers continued to use the ferry. However, by 1914, the track which ran alongside the rails on the bridge was allocated to the use of motor vehicles and pedestrians when no train was on that section of the line and a toll was charged. Demand for the ferry declined until the 1960s when the railway line was discontinued, leaving the bridge open to vehicular and foot traffic, thus finally closing the ferry.

Drove roads from the north converged at the second ferry on Loch Etive which linked the north shore to the village of Bonawe on the south shore. This ferry was complementary to the anchorage there which was used by vessels of small burden carrying cargoes of pig-iron, tanner's bark, kelp and salmon. Moreover, the Lorn Furnace iron-works, established at Bonawe in 1753, brought additional traffic to the ferry. Statute Labour was invoked to improve access roads, particularly the road on the north shore of the loch which leads to the Bonawe quarries. An inn, the ruins of which can

The motor ferry crossing to Ardgour at Corran in 1930 makes a deceptively peaceful picture of the passage over the Corran narrows which could be treacherous.

still be distinguished, was set beside the ferryman's cottage. It was at this inn that McIan of Glencoe stayed on the fateful night of 31st December 1692 when he was on his way to sign the Oath of Allegiance at Inveraray. He slept in his bed uneasy in the knowledge that he had missed the midnight deadline set by the government.

In the nineteenth century, two boats and two ferrymen were employed at Bonawe and travellers such as Dorothy Wordsworth found the service more satisfactory than at many other ferries in the vicinity. She wrote, 'It was pleasing to observe the dexterity with which the lad [ferryman] managed his oars, glorying in the appearance of danger, for he saw us watching him, and afterwards, while he conveyed us over, his pride redoubled; for my part, I was completely dizzy with the swiftness of motion'.

With the influx of motor cars in the twentieth century, the need for larger boats arose, yet, in the 1905 *Contour Road Book*, a warning was given to prospective travellers: 'large boat carries 3 tons; not tried motors yet'. In 1914, the capacity of the boat was increased to ten tons to accommodate vehicles. In the 1930s, a beam-loading vessel, capable of carrying four cars, was used, but in the 1948 review no recommendation was made to develop the service further, and by the 1970s diminishing traffic meant that a small motor launch was sufficient. Today, no regular service is available.

Northwards from Loch Etive, the picturesque beauty of Loch Creran was tempered by the poor quality of the ferry service. The entrance to the loch was guarded by the Shian ferry, a passage of about a quarter of a mile, with the Creagan ferry, only half that distance, located at the opposite end. In the eighteenth century, the rights of these ferries were held by the lairds of Glenure and Airds respectively. In 1733, the Argyllshire Road Trustee Committee decided to replace the Shian and the Creagan ferries by a new ferry to be located at Rugarve with the rights of ferry on the north shore allocated to the laird of Glenure and those on the south shore to the laird of Airds. Such difficulties arose that the Trustees were forced to abandon the idea and revert to the former ferry locations at Shian and Creagan, although facilities there left much to be desired.

In 1803, Dorothy Wordsworth was unimpressed with the amenities at Shian. She described the ferryman's house as being 'so dirty and there were so many wretchedly dirty children . . . a most disgusting combination of laziness and coarseness'. The transport of her horse again proved a problem. She was 'determined not to have the horse in the boat . . . and it was agreed he should swim over. The horse began by pushing under the boat but then he swam easily'. She gave the ferryman '18 pennyworth of whisky' in addition

An ancient ferry plied across the mouth of Loch Long from Dornie to Ardelve. Until well into the twentieth century this ferry was served by an open rowing boat which carried animals as well as goods and passengers. Horses and cattle were difficult to transport as there was little means of controlling them.

to the usual fare as a measure of her relief at her safe crossing.

Lord Cockburn, too, suffered anxiety at Shian. Firstly, delay occurred as the boat, 'although bespoke', was on the wrong side. Then occurred 'the pulling and lifting the poor carriage by Celtic arms alone, unaided by any machinery, the scolding and directing . . . all in Gaelic . . . and no man master!' He added wryly, 'The expeditious passage of a Highland ferry would be a much greater miracle than the passage of the Red Sea!' There was sufficient traffic in the nineteenth century to warrant the building of an inn on each side of the passage. These buildings are now private dwellings. At the beginning of the twentieth century, the ferry boats were incapable of carrying motor vehicles. By 1914, travellers were advised to write in advance to the ferryman at north Shian as there was no boat stationed on the south side; the fare was 1/— per passenger. World War II saw the demise of the Shian ferry, and now only the two old buildings remain as reminders of the important service previously rendered.

An old ferry inn, now upgraded to a luxury hotel, still exists at Ballachulish. This ancient ferry was linked with notorious historical events including the Massacre of Glencoe and the hanging of the Red Fox, together with the commercial business of slate quarrying. In the twentieth century, popular coach and steamer tours made Ballachulish accessible to visitors, but the queues for the ferry became ever longer as more cars were driven to the Highlands. Tourists wanted to explore the countryside that had seen the dark deeds of 1692 when the Campbells had slaughtered the Macdonalds in Glencoe. Lieutenant-Colonel James Hamilton was at the ferry when he received the order to eliminate the Macdonalds. In turn, Hamilton sent a signal to Captain Campbell of Glen Lyon which included the postscript, 'Please order a guard to secure the Ferry and the boats there must be on this syde of the ferry after your men are over'. Thus, a getaway route for the murderers was ensured. Sixty years later, no such escape was possible for James Stewart of the Glen, known as the Red Fox, when he was captured and charged with the murder of Colin Campbell of Glenure, a crime that was never proved. (The episode features in Stevenson's *Kidnapped*.) Nevertheless, he was condemned and was hanged, still protesting his innocence, from a gibbet which overlooked the ferry. The macabre aftermath of this execution was the number of years that the skeleton was left to hang on the gallows where it could be clearly seen from the ferry.

In 1792, the state of the ferry and the inn was the subject of stinging comment by James Lettice, a well-known tourist. He complained that he had to suffer 'a dirty bed, with old

EILEAN DONAN CASTLE AND DORNIE FERRY, ROSS-SHIRE.

In the 1930s, with an increase in the number of motor cars, drivers entrusted even the most expensive and elegant cars to the skills of the ferrymen who worked small, motorised boats. In view of the Eilean Donan Castle, this car is safely aboard the Dornie ferry en route to Ardelve.

sacks and blankets and blocks of wood closing a fissure in the wall' which did nothing to deter 'the wind and rain from entering freely and copiously at the foot of my uncurtained hammock'. He also complained that the boat was too small to convey passengers, horses and carriage in one journey, although an attempt was made to do so. He was 'very anxious' as the horses were afraid and moved about, upsetting the balance in the boat and making the carriage tilt over although the crossing was eventually accomplished safely.

In the early nineteenth century, surveys conducted by Telford and Hope resulted in the construction of new quays but these measures were insufficient, as John MacCulloch wrote to Sir Walter Scott; '. . . it is not justice to say, that the readiness, precision and commodiousness of the Ballachulish ferry confer great credit on the proprietors'. The next hundred years saw little change until May 1906 when the first car was ferried. This operation involved some delicate manoeuvring. The open boat, about fourteen feet long, had two planks placed across it. Then, the car was driven onto the planks to balance precariously. The boat was propelled across the water by the ferryman who wielded two sweeps or long oars, and the fare charged was between 10/— and £1 according to horse-power. Six years later, two motor-turntable ferry boats were introduced, each of which was capable of carrying one car, then charged between 2/6d and 5/— according to length. Not until 1926 was a boat purchased that was able to transport two cars at a time. In spite of the increasing volume of traffic, no improvements were made, so the delays at the ferry became even longer. The 1948 review recommended that a bridge should be built, but instead two new boats, each with a capacity for six cars, were bought. This did little to reduce the queues and an AA guidebook published in the 1950s warned prospective travellers of the congestion.

According to Commander Clark, the last manager of the Ballachulish ferry, the Ballachulish Ferry Company was formed in 1935, taking over from the proprietor of the Ballachulish hotel. Between 1954 and 1969, fares remained constant in spite of increased hours of operation, the trebled number of employees and the provision of six houses, rent- and rate-free, for ferry coxswains. Between 1954 and 1974, the increase in traffic was dramatic, with the number of vehicles carried rising from 42,000 to 204,000. Finally, a bridge was opened on 4th October 1975.

Four miles north of the Ballachulish ferry, the Corran Narrows divide Loch Linnhe from Loch Eil and are still crossed by the Corran ferry. The original ferry passage was located three-quarters of a mile north of the present Ardgour slipway and about one-third of a mile north of the quay on the Nether Lochaber shore. The site was altered when new quays were constructed to accommodate steamboats incorporating a turntable design. In the fifteenth century, the MacMasters held Ardgour but their acquisitive neighbour,

The horn-blower in the picture is re-enacting the role of an 1820 counterpart at Strome Ferry at the mouth of Loch Carron. At that time, mail runners attracted the attention of the Strome ferrymen by blowing a horn when they wished to continue their journey by ferryboat.

Donald McLean, with the support of his father, Lachlan McLean of Duart, attacked and defeated them. After the battle, McLean chased the fleeing chief to the Corran ferry where loyalty to the MacMasters was expected from the ferryman. Instead, the ferryman betrayed his former chief, but in so doing he miscalculated the reaction of Donald McLean, who condemned him for disloyalty and ordered that he be strung from his own oars until dead.

In common with many other ferries, the Corran ferry was of strategic importance. In the 1745 uprising, the garrison at Fort William relied on supplies from Dunstaffnage and Oban. When supply boats sailed through the narrows at Corran, local patriots shot at them. In retaliation, a party of soldiers ransacked and burned the village of Ardgour. This act had repercussions on the lives of those in the surrounding districts of Sunart and Ardnamurchan who were dependent on Ardgour as a centre of communication through the Corran ferry link with the main route to and from Fort William and the north. In 1826, according to Haldane, mail was carried by the ferry three times per week at a payment of £2−12/− per annum; in 1833, this fee was raised to £7−16/− per annum when the postal service between Corran and Strontian was increased to six days per week.

In the 1930s, the McLeans of Ardgour found the upkeep of the ferry a financial burden, so Argyll County Council took it over. Later, the new slipways were built, boats carrying two cars were employed and the fare for one passenger was reduced from 6d to 4d, although cars were still charged between 2/6 and 7/6. Two ferrymen, John Buchanan and James McIntosh, undertook the lease of the ferry for two years until Buchanan retired, leaving McIntosh the sole licensee. In 1945, Peter McQueen was appointed ferryman and held that post until 1974 when he retired following the restructuring carried out by the Highland Regional Council. The recommendation of the 1948 review was implemented in the 1950s when a vessel, able to convey four or five cars, was put on the passage. A similar boat operates at the present time.

Much further north, opposite the island of Skye, the

The Kylesku Ferry on Loch Cairnbawn was, until 1975, the only free ferry in Scotland. The one-car ferryboat in the picture was the forerunner of a larger, modern vessel with a capacity to hold eighteen cars. This boat ran until a bridge was completed in 1984.

Strome ferry had long plied across the entrance to Loch Carron. This ferry was overlooked by an old castle, the domain of the Macdonalds of Glengarry, until 1602 when it was destroyed by the Mackenzies of Kintail. This remote ferry location mainly served local people until 1809 when the Highland Roads and Bridges Commission decided to construct an access road along the north shore of Loch Carron to link up with the Achnasheen to Inverness route. Beset by difficulties, this road took ten years to complete. When Lord Cockburn crossed at Stromeferry in 1820, he exclaimed that 'When our ferrymen were loitering on the south side, it was curious to hear them excited to activity by the mail horn on the other. I had forgot in these solitudes that there was a post'. The ferry, he commented, was 'as well managed as mere hands, without proper boats, piers or any apparatus can ever manage a ferry'. Nevertheless, by that time, there

was at least a regular ferry service which James Hogg found
to be missing on his visit in 1803. No ferry boat being in
sight, Hogg had attempted to hire another boat, bribing the
boatman with 'triple freight'. The boatman, a man of
principle, rejected the offer and Hogg was left standing on
the rocks 'obliged to bellow and wave my hat' to attract the
attention of the legitimate ferryman.

The railway reached Stromeferry in the 1880s and made a
great impact on the volume of traffic at the ferry. The ferry
boat was not designed to cope with such an increase because,
as *Black's Guide to Scotland* warned, 'Horses have to leap from
the pier and it is far from being a safe or an easy means of
transit for horses unaccustomed to such work'. This practice
continued until cars became more numerous in the second
decade of the twentieth century and they were then
transported as at Ballachulish. The 1948 review recommended
the introduction of a turntable and a bigger boat capable of
carrying six cars. This new boat did improve the service
although queues continued to form, especially in the
summer, but somehow the waiting was in keeping with the
general pace of life in these Highland areas. In 1971, the old
road along the north shore of Loch Carron was reconstructed
to renew the route northward to Inverness, thus eliminating
the need for the ferry at Strome.

The last well-known ferry on the west coast is located at
Kylesku on an inlet of Eddrachillis Bay, known as Loch
Cairnbawn. Until the late seventeenth century, this lovely,
remote spot was overlooked by Ardvreck Castle, the seat of
the Macleods of Assynt. Neil Macleod was denounced as a
rebel in the 1672 and the Mackenzies took possession of the
castle and the surrounding land, keeping them for the next
hundred years until the castle was destroyed and the lands
and the ferry passed into the hands of the Sutherland family.
There was no proper road until 1831, so the traveller was left
with the dubious choice of either finding his way over pitfalls
and bogs, or of hiring a boat and embarking on a hazardous
journey among the rocky promontories along the shore. The

The ferry plying across Loch Broom between Ullapool and Aultnaharrie was still in operation in 1988. It was managed by the owners of the Aultnaharrie Ferry Inn, once an ancient hostelry and still a well-known restaurant which attracts many visitors. In this picture, taken in the 1920s, Murdo McGregor, the ferryman, proudly displayed his first ferryboat.

new road was used by a post runner to carry mail once in six weeks and longer in the winter months. Local folk fore-gathered to hear the news he brought.

At the beginning of the twentieth century, boats were kept on the south side of the ferry, and again planks were used on the ferry boat to transport cars. After 1918, a motor boat was employed but this was only available in summer and a yellow flag was flown if there was only a temporary stoppage due to a low tide. A red flag was flown from the south pier if bad weather prevented the ferry from crossing at all. In 1954, two cars could be carried but in 1958 the addition of a turntable meant that this number was doubled. William Brauer, the head ferryman between 1954 and 1984, recalls that the Kylesku ferry was a free ferry, the only one in Scotland, until 1975 when the Highland Regional Council purchased a new boat with a capacity for eighteen cars and a fare of £1.00 per car was introduced. This larger boat was still inadequate and it was agreed that a bridge must be built. In 1984, the completed bridge was opened by the Queen.

Sea-loch ferries, set amid spectacular scenery and operating against the odds dictated by the elements, have an undoubted appeal, both aesthetic and emotional. Ferrymen may have been 'drunken boatmen who keep us for hours in fear and risk our lives or if an insolent or lazy one chooses he can delay us for half-a-day . . .', as John McCulloch said in 1824. Nevertheless, from time immemorial, such men provided the means of transport and communication in remote corners of Scotland. They no doubt tackled the problems they faced according to their abilities and inclination and received scant reward for their efforts. New technology and greater investment have replaced or bypassed the ferries and made the ferrymen redundant. Yet, amid the great rush of progress it is time well spent to visit the old ferry locations and recollect.

CHAPTER 7

Island Ferries

The great tract of sea bounding the west coast of Scotland intersects the land with many channels or sounds. The Sea of the Hebrides and the two Minches flow between the islands of the Inner and Outer Hebrides where unpredictable waters can swiftly be transformed from calm tranquillity to furious turmoil. Many islands are set in the midst of these outreaches of the Atlantic Ocean and, until the introduction of air services, islanders depended on boats for contact with other islands and the mainland. In the past, ferries and other boats provided a vital means of transport, but with the advent of steam regular and reliable ferry services were made possible.

In the Clyde estuary, the main islands, Arran and Bute, are less exposed and less isolated than the islands of the Inner and Outer Hebrides. Brodick, the capital of Arran, is within easy reach of the Ayrshire coast, while Rothesay, the main town on Bute, is separated from the mainland by only two miles of water. In their day, Brodick and Rothesay were each defended by impressive castles. Brodick Castle was part of the dowry of the eldest daughter of James II on her marriage to Sir Thomas Boyd. After divorcing her husband, she remarried and the earldom of Arran, including Brodick Castle, was bestowed on her second husband, Lord James Hamilton. The Hamiltons have retained Arran to the present day and the restored castle is now a great tourist attraction. In contrast, Rothesay Castle, a residence of the kings of Scotland about the twelfth century, was destroyed in 1685 by a brother of the Earl of Argyll and only the ruins remain. Both castles guarded access routes to the two islands and overlooked ferry passages.

The island of Bute was a staging post on the journey

between Glasgow and Kintyre because an established ferry service operated between Kilmichael, on the west coast of the island, and Port-a-chro, about five miles north of Skipness, on Kintyre. This ancient ferry passage, used since the days of the Norsemen and their long boats, continued to meet a variety of needs. In 1802 a Mistress Wynn, who had just married Colin Campbell, the Master of Skipness, travelled to Glasgow in order to purchase a new ball gown. In her diary, this lady related how she and her husband rode from Skipness castle to Port-a-chro. There, they boarded the ferry boat which was of 'large open construction with one sail and four large sweeps [oars] and was operated by four men'. On the boat the couple were accompanied by 'boxes of fish, two goat kids, four rams, one cow and, under cover, ten hogsheads of whisky'. The latter was, of course, illegal cargo. The lady commented dryly, 'My husband remarked that it would be best if we did not meet the revenue cutter on the way over to Bute'. On this occasion, the ferry crew went undetected. Mistress Wynn recounted that on arrival in Bute the boat was met by a horse and gig which took them to Port Bannatyne on the opposite side of the island where they had to stay two days 'to await a boat which was loading potatoes for Greenock', and then the crossing took sixteen hours. On the return journey they had to wait for three days at Kilmichael, lodging in a farm house, until the ferry boat for Skipness arrived. Hopefully, the ball gown was worth all the effort involved. The revenue cutter mentioned by Mistress Wynnn was stationed at Millport on the island of Great Cumbrae, close to the Ayrshire coast. At that time, the captain, James Crawford, his officers and crew, lived on the island from which they made raids to try to curtail the thriving illicit whisky trade.

Another long-established link was the ferry from the village of Kerrycroy, on Bute, to Largs on the mainland where, in 1818, a new boat was put onto the passage. That year there were great celebrations as the islanders rejoiced in the marriage of John Crichton Stewart, Marquis of Bute, to Lady Maria North, daughter of George, Earl of Guildford. A boat, fittingly named *The Lady Guildford*, was built to commemorate the occasion. It was clinker-built and measured twenty-five to thirty feet in length. There was provision for two masts, one for'ard and one amidships but the main propulsion came from eight oarsmen seated side by side wielding oars of hardwood fifteen feet long. The rowlocks for these heavy oars were unusual as they consisted of small square ports sunk into the gunwales. When these ports were not in use they could be blocked by sliding into place small wooden shutters, thus levelling them with the smooth sides of the boat. Mainly passengers were carried on this boat although horses and cattle were put on board. Fares included 4d for a passenger, 8d for a cow when lean at the beginning of summer, with an extra penny being charged when fat at Martinmas. According to information received from George Jarvis of Bute, *The Lady Guildford* was fitted with an engine and a propeller. After the ferry fell into disuse in the 1930s, the boat was preserved and kept in the boatyard of D. McIntyre at Port Bannatyne. Since then, there has been talk of the Maritime Museum at Greenwich being sufficiently interested to include it in an exhibition.

The shortest crossing from Bute to the mainland is from Rhubodach, in the north-east corner of the island, to Colintraive in Cowal. This was an ancient ferry much used by cattle drovers during the great boom in cattle trading in the late eighteenth century. In the twentieth century, traffic at the ferry dropped until, in 1950, the Bute Ferry Company Ltd, under the chairmanship of the Marquis of Bute, was formed and an ex-landing craft started a vehicular service which was developed first by the Caledonian Steam Packet Company Ltd and then by Caledonian McBrayne Ltd. This ferry is still in operation.

The island of Arran, larger and more economically independent than Bute, boasted a number of ferry locations but little of their history is recorded. Brodick and Whiting Bay on the east coast, together with Lochranza in the north and Imachar and Blackwaterfoot in the west, all provided locations for ferry boats. With the advent of steam, a fleet of paddle steamers were employed throughout the Clyde estuary. On Arran, until the late nineteenth century, there was a shortage of piers to serve these steamers, so it was customary for the boats to lie offshore. Passengers had to climb down into small, open, rocking rowing boats to be ferried to land. At Corrie and Pirnmill the old Ferry Rocks can still be seen where passengers scrambled ashore from the rowing boats. Latterly, these small boats were powered by engines and eventually at Pirnmill the last ferryman, Archie Currie, used an old ship's lifeboat to meet the steamers. In 1872, a pier was built at Brodick, and in 1885 another was constructed at Lochranza, permitting passengers and goods to be landed directly.

For years Arran was a centre of whisky smuggling and excisemen found great difficulty in controlling this traffic. At one time, Mary Sillars and her brother, Shaunie, worked a still by the burn above High Banlicken, near Pirnmill on the west coast of the island. They stored the whisky in the byre loft at Banlicken, then transported it down the cart track to Imachar, and finally it was concealed in a smugglers' cave on the shore. When the coast was clear and the ferry passage safe, it was transported across the water to Kintyre. Regular consignments were delivered. One day, in the 1890s, the customs boat was spotted offshore depositing a revenue officer near the beach. Shaunie, who had been acting as lookout, whistled the secret signal to his sister and she hastily removed all the evidence of the whisky before the officer had managed to climb the hill and arrive on her doorstep. Mary agreed to permit him to search the farm house. All went well until he reached a ladder leading to the loft, then Mary took fright and threatened him with an axe while simultaneously fiercely berating him in Gaelic. Terrified, the man fled. He reported that he had found nothing and that all was well. Thereafter, Mary and Shaunie continued happily in their lucrative trade. Another ferry connected

A Clyde paddle steamer leaving Brodick for Ardrossan at the end of the nineteenth century. Brodick pier was built in 1885 and a carriage road was constructed up 'North Glen Sannox and down Glen Chalmadale to the little land-locked bay and clachan of Loch Ranza'.

with the smuggling of whisky operated between Blackwaterfoot and Campbeltown.

In his history of Kintyre, Angus Martin recounts the tale of Lachie Galbraith, ferryman at Port na Cuthaig at Saddell in the 1850s. Evidently, Galbraith hoped to augment his household fare by keeping a pig which unfortunately became a family pet. Eventually, the pig mysteriously disappeared, after which the family were distressed to recognise their erstwhile favourite facing them on the table in the form of succulent joints. Most ferrymen had to eke out a living by running a croft in conjunction with their ferrying, and this often involved keeping livestock.

From 1790, Whiting Bay, on the opposite side of the island, benefited from a regular ferry service to Saltcoats. In 1829, this was superseded by the steamer service from Glasgow, to be followed in 1860 by a direct ferry service from Ardrossan when the railway terminus was built there. Whiting Bay had no pier but there had long been a landing place at nearby King's Cross, so-called because Robert the Bruce left there for Ayrshire when making his bid for the control of Scotland. A pier was erected at Whiting Bay in 1901 but boats continued to call at King's Cross. In the 1920s and 1930s, when pleasure cruises were at the height of their popularity, Whiting Bay pier was in daily use. It was not dismantled until 1964 when the Caledonian-MacBrayne Arran ferry service was reduced to stopping only at Brodick where the drive-on, drive-off *Clansman* still provides five or more daily crossings between the mainland and the island.

The first island off the western seaboard of Scotland is the small isle of Gigha where a ferry operates between Ardminish, the only village on the island, and Tayinloan in Kintyre. This ancient ferry gave rise to some concern in the later eighteenth century because there were no quays at either Ardminish or Tayinloan. In those days, lack of control of the expenditure of funds allocated for road, bridge and ferry maintenance often resulted in misappropriation. In 1763, Malcolm McNeill was allocated 11/4d 'in his hands towards finishing the quay at Gigha', but by 1766, the Commissioners of Supply found that 'no work had been done on the Roads or Quays in that island for some time', so an enquiry was set up. Yet, six years later the Commissioners again authorised McNeill to obtain Statute Labour money from the inhabitants of Gigha to 'build a Quay at the ferrying place near Tayinloan'. Twenty years later, in 1792, the Rev. William Fraser stated in the Statistical Account that 'although there is a regular ferry with two boats, one on the island, the other on the mainland', at least two difficulties remained. These were 'the want of a quay on the Kintyre side, which is much exposed to the storm . . .' and 'the want of a proper house to accommodate people who wait for the ferry', Fraser added, 'It is with regret it must be observed, that such inattention to public convenience has been, and still is, too frequent in the

Highlands'. In 1961, the Third Statistical Account notes that although the pier on Gigha 'has been recently improved by public subscription and free labour . . . there is need for an improved landing stage at Tayinloan'.

Islay, the most southerly of the Inner Hebridean islands, is in close proximity to the island of Jura. The narrow Sound of Islay separates the two islands by only half-a-mile. Islay is a pleasant, fertile island with a number of natural and safe harbours providing easy access, all factors which no doubt influenced the Vikings and Norsemen in their search for protected anchorages. The kings of Man succeeded the Scandinavians as proprietors of the island only to be themselves replaced by the Macdonalds, the Lords of the Isles. The most obvious ferry passage from Islay lay between Port Askaig and Feolin on the south-west of Jura. Other locations, including Port Ellon, Bowmore, Port Charlotte and Portnahaven were also ferry terminals at one time or another.

From the late eighteenth century, the crossing from Port Askaig to Feolin was particularly important as it linked Islay with the black cattle markets on the mainland. The black cattle were not only bred on Islay in their thousands but were gathered there from the outlying islands. The open ferry boat, bow-shaped and cumbersome, was rowed by two or four oarsmen. The comfort of travellers was given little consideration as Thomas Thornton discovered in 1786 on his journey during a *Sporting Tour of Scotland*. He explained how he 'jumped into the boat, alighted on some faggots or hurdles and found myself pretty handsomely splashed with the water which they covered at the bottom of the boat'. It was common practice for ferrymen throughout the Western Isles to cover the bottom of their boats with birch branches, heather or bracken. These served the treble purpose of protecting the wooden floor of the boat, providing a footing for cattle and filtering the cattle dung to prevent the pumps in the larger boats becoming clogged. In 1811, James Macdonald, in his *General View of Agriculture in the Hebrides*,

F

quoted that between 1801 and 1807 the average number of cattle ferried per year from Port Askaig was 2,640. The average price obtained for cattle during that period was £7 per head but the ferrymen received little of the profit in spite of the fact that both owners and drovers depended on their skills.

In 1787, after Islay drovers complained of the lack of a fank for enclosing cattle waiting to be transported, a seventy-acre site was set aside and James Hill was appointed to supervise the management of the cattle. The slipway to the boats was now maintained and cattle could no longer fall and injure themselves. Hill also had to deal with the constant bickering and disputes arising between drovers regarding the order for embarkation for droves sailing for Jura. In 1824, John McCulloch, who was touring the Western Isles described the noise created at the Port Askaig ferry by 'the cattle, some embarking, another set swimming on shore to ferry boats: while the noise of drovers and boatmen and all the bustle and vociferation which whisky did not diminish, were re-echoed from hill to hill, contrasting strongly with the silence and solitude of the surrounding mountains'. In 1818, the Stent Committee of Islay had drawn attention to the unlimited amount of alcohol consumed by ferrymen who were frequently remunerated with a bottle of whisky and, consequently, were in such a state that they proved 'injurious to the cattle and the proprietors thereof'. The Committee decreed that in future the allowance of whisky would be fixed at 'one mutchkin [an English pint] for the first thirty cattle ferried'.

In 1626, the McLeans were the proprietors of Islay and Jura but James VI, irritated by the continued disturbances between the McLeans and other clans, transferred the lands of Islay and Jura to Sir John Campbell of Calder. In 1719, Sir John's successor sold these islands to Walter Campbell of Shawfield who, sixty-one years later, sold Jura to a kinsman, Archibald Campbell. A condition attached to the sale of Jura dictated that fares for cattle on the ferry from Lagg, on Jura,

In the late nineteenth and early twentieth centuries, travellers flocked to visit the Western Isles. The crowds on this single-funnel steamer from Glasgow are disembarking at Port Ellen, on Islay, which was a favourite destination.

to Keills, in Morven, must remain at the fixed rate of five merks per score unless the proprietor of Jura decided otherwise but there was no mention of constructing an access road to the ferry. In 1792, the Rev. John McNeish declared that 'None of the Western Isles can boast of such good roads and bridges as Islay . . . any gentleman may drive for thirty miles through the isle in his carriage'. In contrast, Jura, with the potential for becoming a direct route to the mainland, had no main road from the ferry terminal of Feolin to the ferry at Lagg. This lack of a connection jeopardised the movement of cattle and made communication of any kind a protracted business. The alternative route to the mainland was by packet boat from Port Askaig on Islay to Loch Tarbert in Kintyre, an extensive journey. A new road through Jura and use of the ferries there would have cut the journey by half. Although a new road was eventually agreed in principle by the landed gentry, argument flared when it came to funding.

In 1804, Walter Campbell and Archibald Campbell, together with Archibald McNeill of Colonsay, John McNeill of Oronsay and others, petitioned the Commissioners for Highland Roads and Bridges to build a road between Feolin and Lagg at an estimated cost of £2,000. At last, the Commissioners decided that the arguments in favour of the road outweighed the cost. The road was completed, giving access to the Lagg to Keills ferry and facilitating movement to the mainland. The government was slow to respond to the needs of the islanders, so it was left to those with money to take the initiative and supply their own ferry boats to be run for personal profit as well as for the benefit of the islanders. In 1801, a boat was purchased by five people, each holding an equal share, including the Duke of Argyll, the innkeeper at Scarinish, John Sinclair merchant from Tobermory, the ship's master and Malcolm McLaurie, Chamberlain to the Duke of Argyll in Tiree. The innovation of a post office in Port Askaig at that time encouraged the inhabitants of Islay to correspond to such an extent that the income from the carriage of mail and other goods enabled the boat's proprietors to recoup their initial outlay in an unusually short time.

In his *Agricultural Review*, James Macdonald commented on the demands made on proprietors by saying, 'The proprietor must build quays, he must clean harbours, he must erect bridges and make roads: he must serve and render comfortable the lives of his fellow islanders solely and entirely at his own expense . . . Why? because the island has not by nature the vast advantage of being a national thoroughfare'. McNeill of Colonsay and McLean of Coll both purchased packet boats which served as ferries to Mull. In addition, McNeill built 'an excellent harbour' at Scalsaig on Colonsay. There was competition between proprietors, with the emphasis more on the profit at stake than the welfare of the islanders. Malcolm McLaurine alerted the

The movement of animals, particularly sheep and cattle, to and from the islands and the mainland, as well as from island to island, relied on ferryboats for transportation.

Duke of Argyll to the possibility of greater profit as early as 1802 when he informed the Duke that McLean of Coll 'gives very favourable encouragement to his packet boat and his fare is very low'. Furthermore, the ferryman on the packet boat received 'the grazing of four cows and their followers and a large croft free of rent . . .'. McLaurine urged the Duke to provide a croft 'on easy terms' to the ferryman at Scarinish on Tiree, otherwise, he argued, 'the people of the Island will be induced to go by Coll to Croig in Mull'. James Macdonald recommended that 'the little jealousies and animosities of neighbouring or rival proprietors must be laid aside'. More and better boats would have benefited not only the islanders but those travelling regularly to the islands such as clergymen. A minister often preached in isolated communities, adding expense to inconvenience when two guineas per voyage had to be taken from an annual stipend of only £120.

In the early nineteenth century, the new road on Jura, together with the increase of ferry traffic due to the expansion of the cattle trade, made Lagg an important centre over-shadowing the ancient ferry at Kinuachdrach on the north coast of the island. The Kinuachdrach passage, less dangerous than that at Lagg, failed to attract traffic because there was no access road and travellers had to make their way over rough tracks. Whether or not the ferry at Kinuachdrach should be supported was debated by those with vested interests. In 1764, the proprietors requested permission to remove 'the ferry from Keills to Barrahormid on the Knapdale side and from Lagg to Ardlussa on the Jura side . . .'. No decision was taken by the Commissioners, who blandly asserted that 'the proprietors of Keills and Lagg are appointed to keep good boats and accommodations for passengers and ferrying cattle until the said scheme shall take place and the intended ferry be established'. No change of site for these ferries ever materialised. Three years later, James Campbell of Craignish and Duncan Campbell of Glendaruel, having acquired the tack of both ferries, requested permission to 'sell their boats and discharge the hands' at the Kinuachdrach ferry in order to concentrate on the tack of the Lagg ferry in the hope of capitalising on all developments.

In 1810, those proprietors who had already petitioned for the road from Feolin to Lagg repeated their application to have the Lagg road extended to Kinuachdrach. It was agreed that a 'Bridle road, not exceeding nine or ten feet in width' would be sufficient to meet the likely demand. In 1815, new piers were constructed at both Lagg and Keills, but in 1846, James Mitchell, the eminent civil engineer, was far from complimentary regarding these supposed improvements on Jura. Evidently, he had missed the weekly steamer from Islay and had decided to cross to the mainland from Port Askaig via Feolin and Lagg. He and his companions walked the seventeen miles across Jura to Lagg, arriving there wet and bedraggled. Lagg was crowded with drovers and cattle, as the ferry boats had been delayed by the bad weather. The ferry inn was full of drovers who had been passing the time imbibing whisky. Caring little for such company, Mitchell bribed a ferryman to carry him and his fellow-travellers across the passage, but before they could set sail, a number of drovers, who had had a long wait, were infuriated at the gentlemen jumping the queue and insisted on loading their cattle onto the boat. Eighteen cattle were fastened by their heads to the gunwales on each side of the broad-beamed vessel and the chief drover's horse was put into the middle of the boat. Once into the channel, the boat was forced on by the wind and Mitchell was in terror of its being swamped, especially as the cattle all struggled to free their heads. The ferrymen panicked, and all seemed lost until a drover grabbed the helm and took control. Mitchell expected every moment to be his last but instead they arrived safely at Keills due to 'the gallant Highland drover'. The Lagg ferry fell into disuse with the decrease in the cattle trade, and the only ferry to survive on Jura was from Feolin to Port Askaig. In the 1920s, lighting a fire on the pier at Port Askaig was the only means of hailing the ferry. Nowadays, Jura has surprisingly few visitors for such a beautiful place, perhaps because it can still only be reached by the Port Askaig to Feolin ferry.

The argument continues concerning the benefits of maintaining good internal roads on Jura. In 1987, a newly formed Overland Route Co-Operative proposed that an internal route across the island from Feolin, linking with the Lagg ferry, would not only shorten the journey to the mainland but would also be cost effective. The current Caledonian MacBrayne ferry service between Kennacraig on the Kintyre peninsula and Port Ellon or Port Askaig on Islay takes two hours; then, to reach Jura, there is the additional Port Askaig to Feolin ferry. Consultants have been appointed to determine how future ferry services to Islay and Jura should be routed.

Mull, in keeping with its central position between the outlying islands and the mainland, had at least twelve ferry locations in the early nineteenth century. The three principal ferries operated from Auchnacraig to Barr nam Boc on Kerrera, Ballemeanoch to Keills in Morvern and from Aros to Morvern. Nine smaller ferries ran from Creggan (Crogan) to Lorne, Ardnaugh (Ardnacross) to Kilalintie (Kilundine) in Morvern, Kilninian to Arinagour in Coll, Oskamull to the island of Ulva, Fionnphort to the island of Iona, Ardchoirk to Fiart on Lismore, Craignure to Ardnacroish on Lismore, Fishnish to Lochaline in Morvern and from Balsulanach to Kilerlumkill (Kill) in Morvern. In spite of the choice of ferry, travellers continued to be frustrated by delay compounded by the indifferent attitude of many of the ferrymen. According to the Statistical Account in 1792, 'though the boatmen ferry at times, one cannot force them out but when it suits their humour and convenience, and even then at whatever rates they may please to exact'. Nevertheless, it behoved tacksmen such as John Gregorson, holding the tack of the Auchnacraig inn and ferry, to motivate his ferrymen in order to recoup as much of the £186 annual rent that he paid to the Duke of Argyll, 'the greatest sum paid by any tacksman on the Argyll estates'.

In the late eighteenth century, the Auchnacraig ferry was used almost exclusively to transport cattle, which were collected at nearby Grasspoint from other islands and conveyed to Barr nam Boc on Kerrera. Driven across Kerrera, they then either swam to the mainland across the narrow strait at Dunollie or were boated to Oban. The heavy, broad-beamed, open ferry boats were never adequate to meet the demands put upon them, so ways had to be devised to overcome the problems, and it is surprising that more accidents did not occur. To load cattle on to the boat, a rough block and tackle system was erected on a yard-arm so that each beast could be hoisted aboard. The heads of the cattle were tightly secured to rings on the gunwales. As the ferry approached the landing place at Barr nam Boc, the

Between 1929 and 1973 John MacDonald, Angus MacKechnie and Alec Gibson ran an open motor ferryboat from Fionphort on Mull to Iona. This boat not only carried passengers visiting the island and the Abbey, but it also transported mail, goods and beasts.

cattle were untied and forced overboard to swim ashore. This method, which left dozens of beasts bobbing about in the often choppy waters, did ensure that the cattle were thoroughly washed down after the confines of the boat, and it also enabled the salt in the water to act as a disinfectant on any gashes or cuts they might have suffered in their various struggles.

In 1834, there were four boats at Auchnacraig, two large boats for ferrying cattle, one post sailing boat and a rowing boat for passengers only. These boats were manned by eight men with only four in action at one time. The others were required to be in a state of readiness to come forward if necessary. At Balemeanoch, only two boats were in operation, a large boat for cattle and a small rowing boat for passengers. Between sunrise and sunset, the boats plied back and forth across the passage but at night, when cattle had to be guarded, an extra 3/6d had to be paid to the watchman.

In 1818, the first steam-powered boat sailed through the Sound of Mull, heralding dramatic changes for the Western Isles. By 1821, a regular weekly steamer service was established between Glasgow and Tobermory and between Glasgow, West Loch Tarbert and Port Askaig in Islay. These paddle steamers were objects of awe-inspired curiosity to the islanders, as William Henderson, a steward on the first steamer sailing to Islay, discovered. When the boat docked, few of the local population dared to venture close to this phenomenon, but finally one worthy plucked up enough courage to approach the boat. Henderson was standing on deck holding his pet monkey in his arms, a sight which confirmed the islander's worst fears, as not only had he never seen a steam boat, he had never before set eyes on a monkey. He fled in terror, shouting that it was the Devil himself that worked such a boat.

The romantic scenery and the mysterious allure of the Western Isles attracted the attention of well-known literary figures who undertook the arduous journeys in a spirit of adventure. Dr. Samuel Johnson, James Boswell, the Words-worths, Southey, James Hogg the Ettrick Shepherd and many others not only visited the islands but recorded their impressions, thus acting as excellent public relations agents. The Sound of Mull set the scene for travellers about to gain experience of a different world. On the voyage from Oban, the Lady's Rock would still be visible at low water. It lay before the castle of Duart, the stronghold of the Macleans, and featured in a fifteenth-century incident. It seems that the Maclean of Duart, tiring of his wife, decided to get rid of her but, foolishly, he forgot to take into account her strong family connections: she was the sister of the powerful Earl of Argyll. One night, Maclean abandoned her on the rock, expecting the rising water to drown her and free him. By chance, the unfortunate lady was spotted by a boatload of her Campbell kinsmen as they sailed up the Sound. They rescued her unbeknown to her husband, who assumed she had been drowned and swept away. The Campbells allowed

Maclean to carry out a mock funeral and be lulled into a sense of false security. Later, they took their revenge when one of Lady Maclean's brothers, Sir John Campbell, assassinated him. Thereafter, the rock below Duart Castle was called 'The Lady's Rock'.

The introduction of steam boats boosted the economy of the Western Isles, and on Mull the township of Tobermory thrived from the investments of the British Fishery Company in 1788. Tobermory had always possessed a beautiful natural safe harbour which had served shipping down the ages. In the sixteenth century, a Spanish galleon, the *Florida*, was sunk in Tobermory Bay, apparently by an emissary of Queen Elizabeth, but according to local legend there was another story circulating at the time. It was said that a daughter of the King of Spain once dreamt of a young man so handsome and attractive that when she awoke she decided to search the world to find him. She sailed forth in the *Florida* and eventually reached Tobermory. There she met Maclean of Duart and he fulfilled her dream vision. They fell in love, although Maclean was already married. Maclean's jealous wife appealed to the witches of Mull for help and they responded by casting a spell which effectively sank the galleon and the Spanish princess was drowned. Even today, divers search the spot where the *Florida* went down, but it is gold they seek rather than the remains of a forgotten princess.

Travellers, including Johnson and Boswell on their 1773 tour, visited the smaller islands around Mull such as Ulva, Staffa and Iona. To see Ulva, Johnson and Boswell first journeyed to Oskamull where they 'expected to find a ferry boat but . . . the boat was gone'. Instead, they had to board an Irish packet boat moored nearby. Johnson was intrigued by a tradition peculiar to the island of Ulva. When one of the laird's tenants got married, the laird, MacQuarrie, supplanted the bridegroom and took over the conjugal rights on the couple's wedding night. If the laird was denied this perquisite, he demanded a sheep or a crown piece as a reward for his abstinence. Another example of the inter-

twining of romance and ferries is the well-known tale of
Lord Ullin's daughter. Recounted by Thomas Campbell,
one-time rector of Glasgow University and now buried in
Westminster Abbey, this story concerned the Ulva ferry.
Young MacQuarrie sought the hand of Lord Ullin's daughter
but her father did not consider the young man to be a
suitable match and separated the lovers. One dark and
stormy night, MacQuarrie took the ferry boat down Loch
Keal, captured his beloved and set sail again for Ulva. The
ferry boat had almost reached its destination when it capsized
and sank, drowning the lovers who are said to be buried near
the ferry landing place on Ulva.

Staffa, a tiny island on the sea route from Ulva to Iona, has
remarkable caves which have inspired great poetry and
music. In 1784, Faujas St. Fond, a French traveller, complained that at Staffa 'the landing is especially terrible even
with the smallest boats, so steep is the coast and so furious
the sea . . .'. The ferry boat, he said, was 'very small and
incapable of carrying a sail'. It was rowed by four oarsmen
sitting on benches on either side of the boat. It is difficult,
therefore, to credit the tale of Alan nan Sop, Alan of the
Straws, who, it was said, was born the illegitimate son of a
Maclean of Duart and was conceived in the Staffa ferry boat.
Alan's mother was punished for her misdemeanour by being
made a servant in her father's household while Alan was
despised and neglected, so he took to the seas as a pirate. He
was so successful that he was able to return to Mull to
purchase Torloisk House on Loch Tuan. There he settled
down as a respected and respectable citizen and was
eventually buried on Iona.

From the early nineteenth century, according to the Rev.
Homer, it became 'the custom among the nobility and gentry
of England to include Staffa in their northern excursions . . .'.
The ferrymen were aware of the potential market and reacted
accordingly. As Homer commented ruefully, 'the Highlander
who deals in boats or shelties will take you if he can'. John
Keats and his companion, Charles Brown, had also included

Until Kyle became a railway terminus in 1897 the Glenelg to Kylerhea ferry was the main route to Skye from the mainland. In the twentieth century, the Glenelg ferry continued to sail and Murdo Mackenzie, who became the ferryman in the 1930s, is still well-known in the 1980s. His vehicular ferryboat does a steady trade, particularly in the summer months, with the number of cars being carried greatly outnumbering those transported by the two-car 1952 model.

Staffa in their itinerary. In 1818, they arrived in Oban wet and tired, expecting to find a boat to take them to Staffa, but as Keats wrote to a friend, 'the expense is seven guineas and rather extorted . . . Staffa, you see, is a fashionable place . . .'. Keats and Brown negotiated a fee with the ferryman and succeeded in visiting Staffa. In the late nineteenth century, MacBraynes' royal mail steamers sailed daily by Staffa, but as there were no suitable landing places they had to lie offshore and passengers had to be ferried to the island in small rowing boats. The difficulties of landing on Staffa were eventually met by the purchase of a large red lifeboat, capable of carrying a greater number of passengers. It was manned by experienced boatmen and stationed at the island of

Gometra five miles distant from Staffa. Visitors are still attracted to Staffa and regular excursions are available from Oskamull on Mull and from Oban.

Iona, previously known as Icolmkill, is separated from the Ross of Mull by the Sound of Iona. In 563 AD, St. Columba came as a missionary from Ireland to found a monastery there. Consequently, the island became a place of pilgrimage, and until the mid-eleventh century it was the burial place for many early Scottish kings and chiefs. The powerful attraction exerted by Iona has captured visitors down the ages. A Gaelic proverb asserts that if a man goes once to Iona, he will go three times. The lack of a quay on Iona necessitated Boswell and Johnson being carried ashore on the backs of the Highland ferrymen. Thereafter, they had to sleep in a barn with a portmanteau for a pillow. Such difficulties did little to dissuade people from visiting the island. It was not only an important place in religious terms, its historical importance was emphasised in 1609 when Andrew Knox, Bishop of the Isles, met Highland chiefs there and persuaded them to accept certain measures for law and order which were then recorded in the Statutes of Iona. It has been said that the reverence in which Iona is held is rooted in an ancient Gaelic prophecy translated thus by Dr. Smith of Campbeltown in the late nineteenth century:

> Seven years before that awful day,
> When time shall be no more,
> A watery deluge will o'er sweep
> Hibernia's mossy shore.
>
> The green-clad Islay, too, shall risk,
> While with the great and good
> Columba's happy island shall rear
> Her toes above the flood.

Iona ferrymen worked hard over the years to serve a population which fluctuated between 300 and 500 people. In

1929, Coll McLean, who succeeded his father as ferryman in 1878, was the proud recipient of a presentation acknowledging fifty years' unbroken service. Between 1929 and 1973, John Macdonald, Angus Mackechnie and Alec Gibson operated the ferry boat which was then an open motor-boat carrying not only mail, passengers and goods but cattle too. Today, livestock are transported by steamer direct from Oban and a passenger service plies the short crossing from Fionnphort.

Kerrera, an island in the Firth of Lorn, is divided from the mainland by the Sound of Kerrera which varies from a quarter of a mile to a mile in breadth. This geographical position made the island a convenient stepping stone between the mainland and the islands beyond. There were four ferry locations on Kerrera: Ardmore in the south-west, Barr nam Boc in the north-west, Ardintrive in the north-east, and Port Kerrera in the east. Ardmore and Barr nam Boc linked with Auchnacraig or Grass Point on Mull, while at Ardentrive lay the passage to Dunollie Castle, the stronghold of the MacDougalls of Lorn, and Port Kerrera gave access to Oban on the mainland. In the mid-thirteenth century, Kerrera featured in the plans of Alexander II in his defence against the Norsemen. The King arrived on the island to prepare to lead an expedition against the enemy but developed a fever at Dalrigh or 'the King's field' and died. Later, in 1263, the bay of Oban provided a perfect rendezvous for King Haco of Norway to meet the island chieftains who were his vassals. His own fleet lying in the bay was augmented by over 160 sail. Such an impressive sight must have inspired the king and his forces, but thereafter his journey was ill-fated as he was defeated at Largs and subsequently died in Orkney on his way back to Norway.

The ferries on Kerrera became prosperous in the mid-eighteenth century when thousands of cattle were being exported from the outlying islands. At first, the cattle were transported by a ferry plying from Auchnacraig to Ardmore, but later it was agreed that, due to the increasing number of beasts, Barr nam Boc should also be used as a ferry terminal.

Thus, Ardmore and Barr nam Boc were used as ferry
locations alternatively on a three-monthly rota. This caused
confusion and inconvenience. In 1758, therefore, the position
was resolved by establishing Barr nam Boc as the permanent
ferry site and Ardmore fell into disuse. At the same time, the
Commissioners of Supply authorised the building of 'proper
Quays . . . for ferrying horses and cattle'. The bill rendered
for the building of this quay included items such as, 'Hector
McLean, blaster and quarrier . . . the sum of £3/15/— as
payment for 90 days work at 10d per day'; 'Donald Sinclair,
smith . . . the sum of £2/5/— as payment for 90 days work at
6d per day'; and 'Angus MacIntosh, the sum of 15/— as
payment for 30 days work at the rate of 6d per day'. The life
of this ferry was only about 100 years and its demise was due
to the falling away of the cattle trade together with the
simultaneous expansion of steamer services from Oban. In
1828, a petition from Captain John MacDougall to the
Commissioners of Supply described another problem which
faced the ferrymen and their proprietors. When cattle were
the main concern, it was customary to drive them from Barr
nam Boc to Ardentrive where they then swam the shallow
passage to the mainland at Dunollie. Sheep could not swim
across the passage so, when their numbers increased, the
ferrymen at Auchnacraig bypassed the landing at Barr nam
Boc and took their boatloads of sheep directly to Dunollie.
This adversely affected the livelihood of the Kerrera
ferrymen who complained loudly. In addition, as there were
no fanks at Dunollie, the sheep roamed freely to join
unenclosed cattle, and together they caused great damage to
land and crops. In 1828, cattle proprietors agreed that cattle
would no longer be permitted to swim from Ardentrive to
Dunollie and that instead a ferry boat would be provided to
ship them from Port Kerrera to Oban. However, the Kerrera
ferrymen did not view this agreement with favour and
continued to flaunt their autonomy by swimming their cattle
from Ardentrive to Dunollie. Only later, when the steam
boats transported cattle directly from the islands to Oban,

A traditional method of transporting cattle from the islands was by 'floating' the cattle. The broad-beamed, open ferryboat rowed by four oarsmen towed the cattle across the passage. Three men manned the oars while the fourth sat in the stern and secured the head of the foremost cow.

did the Ardentrive ferry close. Nevertheless, as late as 1973, MacDougall, in his *History of Kerrera*, relates how the Slaterach herd of Highland cattle were ferried across the strait in the traditional manner. Records of the Commissioners of Supply describe the traditional method of ferrying cattle 'by casting down the cattle and tying them in the boats, which cost 8d from 1st January to 1st July when poor and 10d from July to January when fatt of ferry money and a bottle of whisky to the ferrymen every loading'. John MacLaine of Lochbuie proposed a new method whereby the cattle would stand in the boats 'for 1/− each and whisky to the ferrymen as formerly'.

Ferry boats were commonly broad, bulky, heavy and black with pitch. In 1824, a new boat at Port Kerrera consisted of 'not less than a 24 four keel' and the crew numbered 'four men when any black cattle or sheep were to be ferried'. In 1847, the cost of a large boat was £34, a middle-sized boat

£3/10/— and a small boat £1/10/—. The capacity of a large boat was four cows or eight yearlings or fifty sheep. On Kerrera, these boats were beached beside the ferry house, which doubled as an inn, sometimes as a change-house and latterly as a post office. In 1748, according to MacDougall, the ferry house at Port Kerrera was built by John MacMartin at a cost of £4—11—8d. In 1799, the house consisted of the 'Publichouse, kitchen, barn, byre and kiln'. In 1843, a new house was erected. It consisted of two stories, a roof with slates, stairs of red pine, and flooring which was grooved and tongued; the ceiling of the largest room was lathed and plastered, the walls were plastered and the windows were sashed. This must have been a remarkable house for its day on the island. The demise of the Barr nam Boc and Ardentrive ferries, due to the decline of the cattle trade, followed by the depopulation of the island and the generally poor economic climate, resulted in a centralisation of ferry services at Port Kerrera. Little has changed today as the current Kerrera ferry service, in the shape of an open motor launch, operates between Port Kerrera and Oban on a regular schedule.

The island of Lismore, or 'Great Garden', lies in the middle of Loch Linnhe with a ferry passage at the northern tip from Port Ramsay to Port Appin. In the thirteenth century, Lismore was an important ecclesiastical centre with a small cathedral, the ruins of which can be seen today. However, Macfarlane, in his *Geographical Collections*, notes that 'Clanwickgilliechael fell foulf of the last bishop of Lismore and eventually killed him and since that time as yet there has never been a Bishope that did come to Lismore to dwell'. No regular ferry was ever established between the southern part of the island and Auchnacraig in Mull, partly because of the treacherous waters separating the islands and partly because the Auchnacraig ferrymen and tacksmen wanted to maintain a monopoly of ferry services and an autonomy regarding the routes selected. In 1752, these ferrymen were undermined as the inhabitants of Fiart, in the south of Lismore, were being 'pressed into ferrying soldiers stationed in the Garrison of Duart on Mull'. A petition was addressed to the Commissioners of Supply by John Campbell of Cloichombie, either to ban such illegal ferrying or to establish a regular ferry service 'specifying freights and appointing harbours and quays to be made'. Apparently, no action was taken at that time and the unauthorised ferrying continued. It was not until 1789 that the Commissioners acted to prohibit 'all the Tenants, cottars and other inhabitants of Lismore from ferrying from here to Mull any passengers . . .'. Anyone found contravening this decree was to be fined £1. This decision reinforced the status of the Port Ramsay to Port Appin ferry. A passenger boat, now maintained by the Highland Region, still plies that passage. Throughout the summer months a car ferry also operates between Oban and Ardnacroish on Lismore.

Moving northwards, Skye, the largest island of the Inner Hebrides, always well populated, now has a community of about 8,000 people. The proximity of the island to the mainland at both Kylerhea and Kyleakin provides narrow passages of water which can be readily ferried. There was also a ferry passage in use from Ardvasar, in south-west Skye, to Treigh, in south Morar. Treigh was only a beach with no access road, and so ferry passengers had to find their way along the coast to Arisaig, the nearest village, in order to join a road inland. Therefore, when a parliamentary road was built between Fort William and Arisaig, the Skye ferrymen chose to land at Arisaig, thus abandoning the Ardvasar to Treigh route. Of course, when steam boats were introduced in the 1820s, there was a regular stopping place off Arisaig when passengers were ferried ashore in a small rowing boat. In the twentieth century, when the road was extended from Arisaig, through Treigh to Mallaig, the steamers then sailed between Mallaig and Ardvasar, and today this is a car ferry service.

Armadale House, by Ardvasar, for centuries the home of the Macdonald chiefs, was extensively rebuilt in 1801 when

John Spencer-Stanhope, together with Archibald, brother of
Lord Macdonald, paid a visit. The two gentlemen reached
Skye by the Glenelg to Kylerhea ferry, the most frequented
passage at that time. The military road to Glenelg had been
constructed to serve the Bernera barracks, built in 1722, to
house a garrison for the maintenance of law and order after
the 1715 Jacobite uprising. According to Stanhope, they
arrived at the inn at Glenelg exhausted after being exposed
to 'real danger of death by bog, torrent or exposure'. He
added, 'Such is the journey to the Hebrides and none but the
hardy need overtake it'. Another early traveller, John
MacCulloch, recounted his experience at the Kylerhea to
Glenelg ferry in *The Highlands and Western Islands*. In 1819,
he arrived at the Glenelg ferry inn early in the morning to
have breakfast. He ordered tea and eggs from the ferryman's
wife but after a long wait was served with a dirty bowl of salt
herrings and potatoes for which he was charged 2/−. He
had to spend time searching for Nicholson, the ferryman,
and negotiated a price for the ferry fare and for leaving his
horse at the inn. Nicholson's wife accused him of stealing the
horse and threatened to report him to the laird, at which the
price demanded by the Nicholsons for keeping the horse was
increased to 6/−. MacCulloch left disillusioned. Two years
later, however, as he was sailing past Glenelg in a customs
boat, he recounted the story to the revenue officers. Their
immediate reaction was to make for the shore and raid the
inn. They emerged with three caskets of the Nicholsons'
illicit whisky. MacCulloch's revenge was sweet.

   Later, MacCulloch travelled to Arisaig for the ferry to
Ardvasar. Arriving at Arisaig, he found no sign of a ferry
boat, and on enquiring about it he was met with a barrage of
excuses from a group of boatmen: 'There might be a boat, or
not; if there was, it was uncertain if it would carry a horse;
whether it was on this side of the water or the other; whether
it would choose to go or not; whether there was a ferryman;
whether the wind would allow it to go; whether the tide
would suffer it. Furthermore, the ferry boat, if there really

At the railway terminus of Kyle the ferryboat sails over the short distance to Kyleakin on Skye. The prestigious Lochalsh Hotel has long accommodated visitors en route to the island. In recent times, the pier and the ferryboats have been greatly improved to meet the demands of the heavy volume of traffic of the 1980s. In this picture, the smaller ferryboat and modest quay were sufficient to meet the needs of the ferry service in the 1940s.

was one, was miles from Arisaig, somewhere among the rocks and there was no road and no pier' — a reference to the Treigh ferry. Finally, MacCulloch found the ferry boat together with some ferrymen. He told how 'One of these boatmen, half drunk, with his mouth streaming tobacco from each angle, desired to know if I was the gentleman who wished to carry a horse to Skye and invited me to drink a glass of whisky with him'. MacCulloch then asked him, 'Are you the ferryman?' The man replied, 'Na, God forbid I should tak' the bread fra ony man; for, ye see, I belang to the same place and he pays for the ferry, ye ken: he pays rent but his boat canna carry a horse: he has no rigging: but I dinna want to carry you, na, but his boat has nae worth; but I dinna want to tak' awa anyone's bread'. MacCulloch added, 'It was

H

a Sunday and the boats would not put out in any case. On the Monday, the boats were on high ground and would not float until the evening, so a night voyage of fifteen miles on a strong sea with a refractory horse could be anticipated'.

Eventually, MacCulloch boarded the boat which had 'no floor, no rudder, no seat aft, no rowlocks, oars patched and spliced and nailed and a mast without a bolt or haulyards . . .'. Evidently, the rowers soon stopped rowing, the sail could not be hoisted for lack of haulyards. There was no tack or sheet and when the sail was set, it was in the shape of a nightcap and the boat began to go backwards. It seemed that the ferrymen's attitude had changed little since Johnson and Boswell used the Glenelg ferry in 1773 when Johnson was told by the ferrymen that 'a mile on land was two miles at sea'. Boswell remarked that, according to such a philosophy, the twelve-mile journey from Glenelg to Armidale was really only six miles. The ferryman failed to grasp this logic and Dr. Johnson commented, 'Never talk to me about the native sense of the Highlanders. Here is a fellow who calls one mile two and yet cannot comprehend that twelve such imaginary miles make in truth but six'.

It is an accepted principle that change takes place slowly. Certainly, Lord Cockburn, the eminent mid-nineteenth-century judge, found no perceptible evidence of change over forty years at the Kylerea ferry. In his *Circuit Journeys* he recorded that, 'This ferry, though boasted the best in Skye, is detestable, at least for carriages and is as ill-conducted as possible. But what can a ferry be for carriages, where ours is only the third that has passed this year, and the object of the landlord of the ferry house on each side is to detain instead of advancing the passenger, and where, when at last it is seen they can carry it on no longer, the only machinery for putting the vehicle on board consists of dozens of lazy and very awkward Highlanders, all scolding in Erse, who almost lift it and throw it into the groaning boat'.

Between the mid-eighteenth and mid-nineteenth centuries, the Kylerhea to Glenelg ferry had to cope with the great numbers of cattle being sent from Skye to marts in Crieff, Falkirk and the south. Between 5,000 and 8,000 beasts per year crossed this passage. In spite of the fast-flowing, dangerous waters of the strait, the cattle were forced to swim across, albeit at 'slack tide'. An Agricultural Survey of Inverness, dated 1813, described the traditional method used to 'float' the cattle. Drovers 'cut 3ft. lengths of rope, each making a noose one end of which was put under the jaw of every cow, taking care to leave the tongue free . . . Whenever the noose is put under the jaw, all the beasts destined to be ferried together are led by the ferryman into the water until they are afloat, which puts an end to their resistance. Then every cow is tied to the tail of the cow before until, a string of 6 or 8 be joined. A man at the stern of the boat holds the rope of the foremost cow. The rowers then ply their oars immediately . . . The ferrymen are so dexterous that very few beasts are lost'. Nevertheless, a different view was expressed by the Rev. James Hall, writing in Barra in 1807, that this was 'an abominably cruel method . . . and sometimes the beasts drowned or their tails were pulled off'. The Rev. Hall attributed this practice to the indolence of the people, although he did admit that to ship terrified and half-wild cattle in inadequate boats was difficult and dangerous. The cattle trade dwindled in the 1850s and later, in 1897, the Highland Railway Company completed its line to Kyle, thus elevating the importance of the Kyle to Kyleakin ferry while simultaneously diminishing the ferry from Kylerhea to Glenelg. Nevertheless, steady tourist trade to Skye has kept this ferry viable and Murdo Mackenzie, the current ferry-man, has held the post since the 1930s, apart from wartime service. He talks of the spiritual uplift to be gained in spending a lifetime as a ferryman and he still enjoys his job.

The road approaching the ferry quay at Kyleakin is flat and broad and benefits from any comparison with the approach to the Kylerhea ferry. In 1802, Sarah Murray described the access road at that ferry as 'channels made by torrents, precipicies, hollows and rough ways' and 'impossible for horses'. In the nineteenth century, Lord Macdonald contemplated transforming Kyleakin into a considerable seaport, in the same way as other benefactors of the time built 'new towns' on the mainland. Lack of money scotched his plans, although it does seem a pity that no money was invested at least to improve the ferry. Lord Cockburn commented on the state of the ferry in 1841: 'The ferry is still ill provided with a boat and machinery for carriages, but hands, and the hope of whisky did the business, though certainly their knocks and jolts, if survived, are the coach-maker's triumph'.

Kyle became a railway terminal in November 1897, and with the increased numbers of visitors, the Kyle to Kyleakin ferry grew in popularity. Both Kyle and Kyleakin were stopping places for numerous steamer cruises sailing from Portree. Portree flourished in pre-1914 days with cruises to Tarbert, Lochmaddy, Dunvegan, Broadford, Raasay, Staffin, Rodel, Stein, Kyleakin, Kyle, Balmacarra, Glenelg, Isle of Oronsay, Armadale, Arisaig, Eigg, Tobermory, Sale, Loch-aline, Craignure and Oban. Nowadays, while Portree is a port of call, it is no longer a centre for cruises. However, the island of Raasay, traditionally served by a steamer plying between Portree and Mallaig, acquired a regular car ferry service in 1974 which was stationed at Sconcer. This ferry is mainly for the benefit of the Department of Agriculture who own the island, but it has also stimulated tourism, thus improving the economy of a dwindling population. The attractions of Raasay were discovered by Johnson and Boswell when they visited the laird. Johnson recorded that 'The water was calm and the rowers were vigorous: so that our passage was quick and pleasant . . .'. However, he was not so complimentary regarding the landing quay: 'We had, as at all other places, some difficulty in landing, the craggs were irregularly broken and a false step would have been very mischievous'. He went on to analyse the reasons for the lack of a pier: 'But I do not know whether, for many ages, it was not considered as a part of military policy to keep the

In 1982, the latest design of small car ferryboat was commissioned
to sail on the ferry passage between Sconser, on Skye, and the
island of Raasay, thus providing easy access for visitors and workers
going to the island.

country easily accessible. The rocks are natural fortifications
and an enemy climbing with difficulty, was easily destroyed
by those who stood above him'. Boswell, more concerned
about the ferrymen, described them as 'four stout rowers,
particularly a Macleod, a robust, black-haired fellow, half-
naked and bare-headed, something of a wild Indian and an
English tar'. As Johnson declared, 'This is a truly patriarchal
life', but this disintegrated after the financial decline of the
Macleods of Raasay, to the point where the island had to be
sold to a wealthy Edinburgh man in 1846. He immediately
cleared the land of 120 families and replaced them with
sheep. Perhaps a new modern ferry boat will ensure long-
term financial stability on the island.

Another little known and ancient ferry place on Skye lies at Ashaig. This ferry was made famous by St. Maolrubha, a holy man who preached at that spot. It was said that he kept his holy books in a cleft in the rocks and hung a bell on the branches of a nearby tree. Ashaig still plays its part in a modern form of ferry service, as it is now the site of the airstrip on Skye.

Reliance on ferry boats, not only for the carriage of people and goods, but for the transmission of news, gave these services a prominent and vital place in the life of the island. Ferry services were constantly under scrutiny, therefore, and were often severely criticised, but without any attempts being made to improve the service. In 1814, Robert Heron, in his *Agricultural Review*, commented that 'Ferry boats are too few, too uncertain and irregular'. He pleaded, 'Let packet boats, post offices and post boys be industriously multiplied'. The nineteenth-century response to this plea came in the shape of MacBrayne when, in 1879, David MacBrayne continued and expanded the steamer ferry services he had begun earlier with his partner David Hutcheson. Glasgow to Portree and, further, to Lewis, Harris, North and South Uist and Barra formed a network of ferry services with Uig, on Skye, the ferry terminal from the Outer Hebrides. In the eighteenth and nineteenth centuries, shiploads of cattle and kelp from the Outer Hebrides arrived at Uig to be transported across Skye to the mainland. In the nineteenth and twentieth centuries, MacBrayne's steamers sailed daily from Uig to the islands and in 1964, the introduction of a car ferry ensured that the ferry traffic at Uig continues to flow.

The service provided by these steamers failed to meet the needs of some smaller Hebridean islands. The transportation of beasts was a constant problem and, traditionally, this difficulty was solved by swimming them across the passage. Even in the twentieth century, the islanders of Vatersay, separated from Barra by three hundred yards of water, expected some assistance in procuring the services of a bull. By custom, the local open-deck ferry boat towed a rowing

This 60-ton cutter, the *Perseverance*, sailed from Lochmaddy, on North Uist, to the islands of the Outer Hebrides. It averaged five round trips per week throughout its run of ten years and carried mail between Lochmaddy and Barra, South Uist and Benbecula.

boat to which the bull was attached by ropes. With the help of diesel and oar power, the bull was able to swim across the Sound. This tried and tested method fell into disrepute in 1987 when Bernie, a prime Aberdeen-Angus bull, died immediately after crossing, to the dismay of those concerned. Although a prosecution ensued, the sheriff found 'no evidence which led him to believe there was anything wrong in using this method to transport cattle'. Indeed, a second bull, Hector, successfully swam the Sound to fulfil his predecessor's mission. Therefore, an ancient custom was legally preserved, but perhaps the islanders of today might have welcomed the building of a causeway between the islands, as it has been argued that such a structure would guarantee the long-term existence of the island community.

In Skye, the black hulls and scarlet funnels of the MacBrayne steamers, now Caledonian-MacBrayne Ltd., are at present augmented by the limited air service which Loganair operates from Ashaig. The only other change mooted which could influence communication between Skye and the mainland would be the building of a bridge between Kyleakin and Kyle of Lochalsh. Arguments, both for and against such a proposition, have been rife for years. A similar situation was experienced prior to the building of each of the important road bridges over the Rivers Clyde and Forth and the Moray and Cromarty Firths when the money necessary to implement plans was not forthcoming for many years. In 1969, a feasibility study estimated that a suspension bridge joining Kyle and Kyleakin would take three years to build at a cost of £2.9 million and would carry about 200,000 vehicles a year. At that time, the Highlands and Islands Development Board decided that instead new ferry boats would suffice, so travellers and locals alike had to be content with the introduction of roll-on, roll-off boats. These still do not eliminate tedious queues of cars in the summer months.

The quality of communication links greatly influenced the mutual prosperity and social interaction of islanders and those on the mainland. In the past, travellers, using the available ferries to reach the islands, would surely have had to subscribe to Robert Louis Stevenson's philosophy regarding travel, 'To travel hopefully is better than to arrive', and 'I travel not to go somewhere but to go'. The widespread romantic notion attached to being transported by ferry boat to these most beautiful of islands might in reality have proved to be a harsh, frustrating and uncomfortable experience, but this did not deter the romantics. Even travelling on present-day ferries, so safe, speedy and convenient, gives the visitor to the Western Isles a feeling of adventure and a sense of stepping into a different world.

Ferries Still Operating in Scotland and the Islands in 1988

Ardrossan to Arran.
Badlurach over Little Loch Broom.
Cape Wrath to Orkney.
Castle Levan to Kirn/Hunter's Quay.
Claonaig to Lochranza (Arran).
Colintraive to Rhubodich (Bute).
Corran Ferry over Loch Linnhe.
Cramond Ferry over the River Almond.
Cromarty to Nigg.
Cuan Ferry from Seil to Luing.
Fionnphort to Iona.
Fishnish to Lochaline.
Fort William to Camusnagaul.
Glenelg to Kylerhea.
Gourock to Dunoon.
John O'Groats to Orkney.
Kennacraig to Islay.
Kyle of Lochalsh to Kyleakin.
Lagg (Jura) to Keillmore (Knapdale).
Largs to Great Cumbrae.
Lochaline to Ardtornish.
Mallaig to: Armadale (Skye).
     Canna.
     Eigg.
     Muck.
     Rhum.
Oban to: Barra.
   Coll.
   Colonsay.

Kerrera.
Lismore.
Morvern.
Mull.
Tiree.
Uist.
Port Appin to Port Ramsay (Lismore).
Port Askaig (Islay) to Feolin (Jura).
Port of Monteith to islands on Lake of Menteith.
Rowdennan to Inverbeg on Loch Lomond.
Rothesay (Bute) to Wemyss Bay.
Sconser (Skye) to Suisnish (Raasay).
Scrabster to Orkney.
Tayinloan to Ardminish (Gigha).
Tobermory to Kilchoan.
Uig (Skye) to: Outer Hebrides.
               Tarbert.
Ullapool to' Altnaharrie.
               Stornoway.
Whitehouse (Mull of Kintyre) to: Ardminish (Gigha).
                                  Port Askaig (Islay).
                                  Port Ellen (Islay).

Scottish Ferries Down the Ages

Abbey St. Bathana
Abbotsford
Abbotshaugh
Aberdour
Aberfeldy
Abergeldie
Aberlour of Skirduston, Boat of
Aboyne or Bontie or Bowntie or Bonte, Boat of
Aigas
Aikenway
Aird
Alcaig
Alford, Boat of
Allanaquoich Boat
Allanbank
Alloa
Alltdourie Cottage Boat
Alness
Alyth
Ancrum
Annan
Annan (Seafield)
Ardchattan
Ardearg, Boat of
Ardentinny
Ardentrive
Ardeonaig
Ardgowan
Ardgulich
Ardminish
Ardmore

Ardnacross
Ardnaugh
Ardneachdie
Ardpatrick
Ardrossan
Ardyne or Port Lamont
Arinagour
Arisaig
Armadale
Aros
Ashfield
Askaig, Port of
Auchenlochan
Auchinbody
Auchnacraig

Badd
Badlurach
Bailemeonach
Balblair or Inverbreakie
Baldayde, Bieldside, Boldside, Boleside
Ballachulish
Ballater
Ballinluig
Balloch, Boat of
Balmackneill
Balmaghie, Boat of
Balnaferry
Balnellan
Banavie
Banchory (Devenick)
Banchory (Ternan)
Banff
Barpuntaig
Barr nam Boc
Barswick or Burwick
Bearscrofts

Beauly
Bermonie or Bardmony (on the River Isla)
Bighouse
Birse, Waterside of
Black's Boat (on the River Spey)
Blackwaterfoot
Blairmore or Portinstuck
Blair's Ferry (River Dee)
Blair's Ferry (Kyles of Bute)
Boat of Bridge or Boat of Brig
Bog, Boat of, or Gight, Boat of, or Fochabers
Bonar
Bonawe
Bo'ness or Borrowstounness
Bonhill
Bonnavoulin
Bowden
Braemar, Castleton of
Brandy Ferry
Bridge-end
Bridge of Earn
Broomielaw
Broughty Ferry
Budge, Boat of
Bullwood
Burnmouth Ferry
Burntisland or Kinghorn Wester

Cairndow
Cambuskenneth
Cambus o' May
Campbeltown
Caolas
Cape Wrath to Orkney
Caputh
Cardross (Clyde Estuary)

Cardross (River Forth)
Carey
Cargill
Carlops
Carlowrie
Carmichael
Carpow
Cashel Dhu
Castlebay
Castle Levan to Kirn/Hunter's Quay
Chanonry or Ardersier or Fort George
Chapell Ferry
Charleston
Clachan on Loch Tarbert
Cladich
Claonaig to Lochranza (Arran)
Cloch
Cluny Ferry (River Ore)
Clydesholme
Cobble Hole
Coldstream
Colintraive
Comrie
Conan
Connel
Corehouse
Corran
Cortleferry
Cothall
Coulport
Coupar-Angus
Coustonn
Craig
Craigellachie
Crailing
Cramond
Crathes

Crathie
Creagan, or Cregan, or Crigan
Cree, Ferry town of
Creggans (Strachur)
Crinan
Croggan or Creggan
Cromarty
Cromdale
Crook-Boat
Crossford
Cuan Ferry from Seil to Luing
Cullnamune
Cupar

Dalpatrick
Dalmaik
Dalreoch
Dalserf
Dalvey
Darnick or Darnwick
Delnapot
Dennily, Miln of
Dingwall
Dinnet, Boat of
Dog's Ferry
Doirlinn
Dollery
Dornie
Dornoch
Doune
Downcraig
Drip
Drum, Mills of, East Boat
Drum, Mills of, West Boat
Drum, Nether Mill of
Dryburgh
Drymen or Catter

Duirinish
Dumbarton
Dun
Dunagoil
Dundee
Dunkeld, East
Dunkeld, West
Dunlugas
Dunollie
Dunoon
Dunvegan
Durris
Dysart

Earlsferry
Elchies Wester
Ellon
Erskine
Eskadale
Ettrick
Eynort

Farr
Feolin
Fernish or Rhemore
Ferrar, Boat of
Ferryhill
Ferry Port-on-Craig (Tayport)
Feugh, Boat of
Fiart
Fiddich, Boat of
Findhorn
Fionnphort
Fishnish
Fonab
Forteviot
Fortingall

Fort William to Camusnagaul
Foulis
Frew
Furnace

Gartartan
Garten, Boat of
Gatehouse-of-Fleet
Glenborrodale
Glenelg
Glenfinnan
Glen Tanar Church
Gourock to Dunoon
Govan
Grange Pow Ferry
Granton
Grantown-on-Spey
Gribon

Halyard Ferry (River Isla)
Hatton, Boat of
Haughhead
Haughton
Heilam
Helmsdale
Heugh-head
Higgins Neuk or Airth
Hoddam
Hope
Horncliff
Huna or Houna
Hunter's Quay

Imachar
Inchbars, Boat of
Inchinnan
Inchmarlow, Boat of

Inchyra
Innerpeffray
Insh, Boat of
Insh of Culter
Inver (River Dee)
Inver (River Tay)
Inveraray
Inverbeg
Invercauld, House Boat of
Inverchandlick
Invercoe (River Coe)
Inverdruie
Inverdunning, Boat of
Invergordon
Inverkeithing
Inverkip
Invermay
Inveruglas
Inverurie, Boat of
Iona
Irvine
Islandurinish

John o' Groats

Keil
Keils or Keill or Keills or Keillmore
Keithhall, Boat of
Kelso
Kemnay, Boat of
Kenmore
Kennacraig to Islay
Kennerty
Keodale
Kerrycroy
Kersie
Kessock, North

Kessock, South
Kilchoan
Kilchrenan or Portchrenan
Killbeg
Killundine
Kilmichael
Kilmun
Kilvichocharmaig
Kincardine o' Neil
Kincarrathie
Kinchirdie or Kinchurdy
Kinclaven
Kinfauns
Kingairloch or Camasnacroise
Kinghorn
Kingussie
Kinlochrannoch
Kinnaber
Kintore, Boat of
Kinuachdrach
Kirkcaldy
Kirn
Knock
Kyleakin
Kyle of Loch Alsh
Kylerhea
Kylesku

Ladykirk
Lagg
Lairg
Lakersaig, Port-na-
Lampits
Langholm
Langlands
Largo
Largs to Great Cumbrae

Leith
Leny
Lesmahagow
Leven, Loch (Kinross)
Liddesdale
Lindores
Little Ferry
Livingstone, Boat of
Lochaline to Ardtornish
Lochawe
Lochboisdale
Lochgilphead
Lochmaddy
Logierait, Boat of
Lorn
Luss
Lyon, Loch

MacDougall's Boat (on the River Dee)
Madderty (River Earn)
Mallaig to Armadale
Meigle
Meikle
Menteith, Port of
Millheugh
Millport
Monaltrie
Montrose
Monymusk
Moulin
Moy, Boat of

Nairn
Newhaven
Newlands
Newport
Newstead

Newtons Ferry
North Berwick

Oban
Onal (River Awe)
Orchard
Otter, Easter
Otter, Wester

Perth
Peterculter
Pettycur
Pitnacree
Point House
Polhollick
Poolewe (on Loch Maree)
Poolewe (to Stornoway)
Port Allen
Port Ann
Port Appin
Port Kerrera
Port of Menteith
Port Ramsay
Portchrenan or Kilchrenan
Portencross
Portincaple
Portindornoch
Portinlick
Portinnisherrich
Portnacraig
Portsonachan
Potarch
Preston

Queensferry, North
Queensferry, South

Rannoch, Loch
Renfrew
Reraig (Loch Alsh)
Rhemore or Fernish
Rhone, Boat of (Loch Ken)
Rhu or Row
Rhynd, Easter
Roan, Boat of
Roberton
Rosehall
Rosemarkie
Roseneath
Rothesay
Rothiemurchus
Rowardennan
Rownacairn
Roxburgh
Rugarve
Rutherford

St. Catherine's
Saddell
Scalasaig
Scaniport
Scaranish
Scatwell, Milltown of
Sconser
Scoulag
Scrabster to Orkney
Scuddale
Selkirk
Shian or Shean
Shillshill
Silvercraigs
Skarfskerry
Skipness
Spatt's Carn

Sprouston
Stenhouse
Stirling
Stornoway
Strachur (Creggans)
Strome Ferry
Strontian

Tain
Tarbet
Tarbert (Island of Harris)
Tarbert, East (Kintyre)
Tarbert, West (Kintyre)
Tarbert (Loch Fyne)
Tay, Loch
Tayinloan
Tayport (Ferry Port-on-Craig)
Tayvallich
Thankerton
Thornhill
Thurso
Tibbers
Tinwald
Tobermory
Tongue
Torry
Totaig across Loch Dunvegan, Skye
Troqueer
Trossachs
Tullich, Boat of
Tulliford or Tullieford
Tummel

Uig
Ullapool
Ulva

Unes
Urray, Boat of

Wark
Waulkmill
Wester, Loch of or Wester Water
Westhouses
Whitehouse (Mull of Kintyre) to Gigha and Islay
Wick
Woodhaven

Suggested Further Reading

Burt, Edward, *Letters from a Gentleman in the North of Scotland to his Friend in London,* 2 vols. (London, 1754)

Cockburn, Henry (Lord Cockburn), *Circuit Journeys* (Edinburgh, 1888)

Cooper, D., *Road to the Isles* (London, 1979)

Fenton, A. and Stell, G. (eds.), *Loads and Roads in Scotland and Beyond* (Edinburgh, 1984)

Fraser, G. M., *The Old Deeside Road* (Aberdeen, 1921)

Gaskell, P., *Morvern Transformed. A Highland Parish in the Nineteenth Century* (Cambridge, 1968)

Gauldie, Enid, *The Scottish Country Miller, 1700–1900* (Edinburgh, 1981)

Graham, Henry Grey, *The Social Life of Scotland in the Eighteenth Century,* 2 vols. (Edinburgh, 1899)

Grant, Elizabeth, *Memoirs of a Highland Lady, 1797–1827* (London, 1898)

Haldane, A. R. B., *The Drove Roads of Scotland* (Newton Abbot, 1952)

Haldane, A. R. B., *New Ways through the Glens* (Newton Abbot, 1962)

Hogg, James, *Highland Tours* (Hawick, 1981)

Mitchell, Joseph, *Reminiscences of My Life in the Highlands,* 2 vols. (London, 1883, 1884)

Smout, T. C., *A History of the Scottish People, 1560–1830* (London, 1969)

Wordsworth, Dorothy, *Recollections of a Tour made in Scotland in 1803* (London, 1874)

Index